David

Thank you!

Mark

The SAFE Leader

Engineering Inclusive Cultures

DR. MARK MCBRIDE-WRIGHT, MBE, CEng, MIChemE

Founder & CEO, EqualEngineers

Royal Academy of Engineering Visiting Professor,
Inclusive Engineering Leadership at
Centre for Engineering Education,
University College London

Copyright © 2024 Dr. Mark McBride-Wright. All rights reserved.

No part of this publication shall be reproduced, transmitted, or sold in whole or in part in any form without prior written consent of the author, except as provided by the United States of America copyright law. Any unauthorized usage of the text without express written permission of the publisher is a violation of the author's copyright and is illegal and punishable by law. All trademarks and registered trademarks appearing in this guide are the property of their respective owners.

For permission requests, write to the publisher, addressed "Attention: Permissions Coordinator," at the address below.

Publish Your Purpose
141 Weston Street, #155
Hartford, CT, 06141

PYP **Publish Your Purpose**

The opinions expressed by the Author are not necessarily those held by Publish Your Purpose.

Ordering Information: Quantity sales and special discounts are available on quantity purchases by corporations, associations, and others. For details, contact the publisher at hello@publishyourpurpose.com.

ISBN: 979-8-88797-072-1 (hardcover)
ISBN: 979-8-88797-073-8 (paperback)
ISBN: 979-8-88797-074-5 (ebook)

The information contained within this book is strictly for informational purposes. The material may include information, products, or services by third parties. As such, the Author and Publisher do not assume responsibility or liability for any third-party material or opinions. The publisher is not responsible for websites (or their content) that are not owned by the publisher. Readers are advised to do their own due diligence when it comes to making decisions.

Publish Your Purpose is a hybrid publisher of non-fiction books. Our mission is to elevate the voices often excluded from traditional publishing. We intentionally seek out authors and storytellers with diverse backgrounds, life experiences, and unique perspectives to publish books that will make an impact in the world. Do you have a book idea you would like us to consider publishing? Please visit PublishYourPurpose.com for more information.

ABOUT THE AUTHOR

Dr. Mark McBride-Wright, MBE, CEng, MIChemE
Founder & CEO, EqualEngineers
https://www.linkedin.com/in/markmcbridewright/
mark@equalengineers.com

Dr. Mark McBride-Wright, MBE, CEng, MIChemE, is a recognised diversity and inclusion leader. He is the recipient of the prestigious Rooke Award from the Royal Academy of Engineering in July 2022 for his work in promoting engineering to the public. In June 2023 he was awarded an MBE for services to Diversity, Equity, and Inclusion in the King Charles III's Birthday Honours. He is a Visiting Professor of Inclusive Engineering Leadership at University College London.

He is Founder and Chief Executive Officer of EqualEngineers, a company offering a wide array of diversity and inclusion consultancy and training services, as well as creative events. Mark has delivered over fifty Engineering & Technology careers fairs since 2017, connecting over 10,000 diverse opportunity-seekers with over one hundred inclusive employers. Mark also founded the Equality in Engineering conference and the Engineering Talent Awards, and established the Masculinity in Engineering research theme leading to a new way to deliver more impactful positive interventions on organisational culture change. EqualEngineers has trained thousands of engineers on creating inclusive cultures from front line leaders and operatives to senior leadership and executive teams. Clients include EDF Energy, SSE, Eurostar, GKN Aerospace, and Institution of Mechanical Engineers, amongst others.

Mark cofounded InterEngineering, a cross-industry network that connects, informs, and empowers LGBTQ+ engineers and supporters. In recognition of his diversity work, Mark won the coveted Corporate Rising Star award at the 2016 British LGBT Awards and was ranked #2 in the 2015 Financial Times Future LGBT Leaders list (#6 in 2016). In addition, he was "Highly Commended" at the Inclusive Networks Awards (2015), shortlisted for the Corporate Equality Award by PinkNews (2016), was listed in the 2023 LGBTQ+ Trailblazer List from Attitude, and was shortlisted in the Top 10 Outstanding Contribution to LGBTQ+ Life at the 2023 British LGBT Awards.

He has worked with many Fortune 50 companies on D&I programs and talent engagement strategies and has also authored a white paper for the UK Government on tackling homophobic, biphobic, and transphobic bullying in engineering. Mark is a Chartered Engineer (IChemE) by training with a focus on Health & Safety, having worked at KBR Inc. (2013–2017) and ERM (2012–2013) before pursuing his work in diversity. He also holds a doctorate (PhD) in chemical engineering at Imperial College London (2009–2013).

Starting to read

The
SAFE
Leader?

Take a picture with the book and use the hashtag to get yourself spotlighted!

#TheSAFELeader

@equalengineers

www.equalengineers.com

TESTIMONIALS

"The SAFE Leader is an important catalyst to stimulate debate. It is also refreshing to see recognition of the need to include everyone, including majority groups as well as minorities. Whether you are an engineer, a Health & Safety professional, an educator, or simply a concerned citizen, I believe you will find food for thought and ideas which will resonate."

—Dame Judith Hackitt DBE, FREng, FIChemE, FCGI, Former Chair of the UK Health & Safety Executive

"The SAFE Leader masterfully bridges theory and practice, offering a compelling vision for a future where everyone belongs. Dr. Mark McBride-Wright's leadership experience and lived experiences are critical to the message delivered in this book."

—Paul E. Wolfe, Former Chief Human Resources Officer, Indeed.com, Human First Leadership Advocate and Author of *Human Beings First*

"An indispensable guide for leaders and teams, The SAFE Leader offers a profound roadmap to fostering true belonging and innovation in the modern workplace."

—Jennifer Brown, WSJ Best-Selling Author of *Inclusion*, *Beyond Diversity*, and *How to Be an Inclusive Leader*

"Insightful, honest, and a necessary call to action, The SAFE Leader is the blueprint every organization needs to unearth the true potential of its people. Dr. McBride-Wright is a justice warrior and thought leader who is changing the world."

—Erin Weed, Founder of The Dig

"The SAFE Leader brilliantly equips readers to speak, act, and lead with authenticity, fostering environments where everyone truly thrives."

—Eduardo Placer, Founder, Fearless Communicators

"Scientists and engineers need this book! With clarity and conviction, The SAFE Leader illuminates the path forward for organizations seeking genuine inclusivity and growth."

—Dr. Sallie E. Greenberg, Affiliated Principal Research Scientist, Illinois State Geological Survey

TABLE OF CONTENTS

About the Author v
Testimonials ix
Glossary of Terms xv
Foreword xvii
Mission Statement xxi
Dedication xxiii
Acknowledgments xxv
Content Warning xxvii
Preface – Guidance Notes xxix
Introduction xxxi

Chapter One 1
Diversity, Equity, and Inclusion: Foundations and How This Links to Safety in Engineering
    What Is Diversity, Equity, and Inclusion? 1
    The Importance of Diversity, Equity,
    and Inclusion 3
    Linking Health & Safety with Diversity,
    Equity, and Inclusion 14
        Workplace Injuries 14
        Key Takeaways 16

Chapter Two 17
How the Operating System was Built: The History of Physical Safety in Engineering
    The Industrial Revolution, *1760–1800s* 19
    The Factory Act, *1802* 20
    The Introduction of Factory Inspectors, *1833* 22

The Introduction of Duty of Care, *1832* 24
Safety Regulations Increase, *1842–1878* 26
The Employer's Liability Act, *1880* 29
A Continued Increase in Acts and Reforms,
1880–1970s 31
 Occupational Safety and Health Act
 (United States), *1970* 32
 Health & Safety at Work Act, *1974* 35
2010s and Beyond 37
Modern Physical Safety 37
 Lost Time Incident Rates (LTIRs) 37
 The Bradley Curve 39
 Organisational Responsibility 40
 Stop Work Authority Cards 41
 Identifying the Difference
 Between Hazard Types 43
Key Takeaways 45

Chapter Three 47
**SOS: The Failure of the Current Safety
Operating System**
Covid-19's Impact on the Engineering Workforce.... 48
 Case Study 50
Trusting Teams 55
Diversity Reboots Outdated Operating Systems 62
Inclusive Engineering Design 65
Key Takeaways 70

Chapter Four 71
**Expanding the Operating System to Include
Psychological Safety**
Improving Mental Health and Well-Being and
Reducing the Risk of Suicide Through DEI 71
Mental Health First-Aiders 73
Destigmatising the Discussion around
Mental Ill-Health 76

Mental Health and Psychological Safety................ 77
The SAFE Leader© Model 82
Unconscious Bias... 83
    How DEI Tackles Unconscious Bias................. 87
The Importance of Equality
for Psychological Safety..................................... 91
The Importance of DEI for Psychological Safety 92
    Recommendations: How to Improve
    Mental Health in the Engineering Sector 93
Key Takeaways.. 95

Chapter Five 97
A New Inclusive Operating System:
The Bradley Curve Revisited

1) Culture: Reactive – Motivation:
   Natural Instinct 99
2) Culture: Dependent – Motivation:
   Supervision.. 100
3) Culture: Independent – Motivation: Self.......... 101
4) Culture: Interdependent – Motivation:
   Teams 102
Reactive vs. Interdependent Culture................... 103
The Bradley Curve and Psychological Safety 105
    Case Study... 109
Concept: Stage 5 – Inclusive Interdependence©... 114
    The Allyship Paradox................................. 114
Key Takeaways... 118

Chapter Six.. 119
How Diversity, Equity, and Inclusion, and Health
& Safety Interlink to Create Psychological Safety

The Groupthink Paradox 121
Merging H&S and DEI...................................... 122
Psychological Safety Attracts Fresh Talent 124
Key Takeaways... 130

Chapter Seven 133
Engaging the Majority: Masculinity in Engineering
   Men's Engagement.. 134
   Men as Allies... 137
   How to Embed DEI in Male-Majority Teams
   and Save Lives 139
      Inclusive Leadership 139
      Self-Development 142
      Recognising DEI is People-Led..................... 143
      Managing Diversity 146
   Bystander Training.. 147
   ALGEE Training... 151
   ASIST Training 152
   Key Takeaways... 154

Conclusion.. 155
The Future of Engineering:
A System that Works for *ALL*!
   Next Actions 159
Bibliography 165

GLOSSARY OF TERMS

Cisgender	denoting or relating to a person whose gender identity corresponds with the sex registered for them at birth; not transgender.
Transgender	denoting or relating to a person whose gender identity does not correspond with the sex registered for them at birth.
Neurotypical	not displaying or characterised by autistic or other neurologically atypical patterns of thought or behaviour.
Neurodivergent	differing in mental or neurological function from what is considered typical or normal (frequently used with reference to autistic spectrum disorders); not neurotypical.

FOREWORD

As a fellow chemical engineer and the former Chair of the UK Health & Safety Executive, I am delighted to provide the foreword for this thought provoking work, *The SAFE Leader: Engineering Inclusive Cultures*.

My own journey in the fields of engineering and safety has been a road of continual learning, intricate problem-solving, and dedication to building secure and inclusive environments for everyone involved. Reflecting on my time spent in the chemical industry itself I am reminded of the journey I was part of to get the industry itself to consider the environmental impacts of its products in use and disposal – recognising that inclusion meant considering those in the whole supply chain not just the direct workforce. At the UK Health & Safety Executive, I am reminded of the depth and breadth of the issues we tackled and the significant role that the diversity of perspectives played in our successes – especially in getting health onto the agenda alongside safety.

Mark brings much-needed attention to several aspects of STEM which are often overlooked but which are fundamentally vital: the intersection of culture, masculinity, mental health, and safety. It is a brave endeavour to delve into these interconnected issues and provides us all with much needed food for thought and reflection.

Inclusivity is a key ingredient in the recipe for progress. Diverse viewpoints provide a more holistic understanding of problems and fuel innovative solutions. This book eloquently advocates for creating an environment that embraces diversity and inclusivity, leaving no one feeling left out or marginalised, and providing a stage for every voice to be heard, respected, and valued.

For too long we have shouted "safety" and whispered "health" and it is clear that mental health is an essential part of what we must speak up about. Feeling safe to speak about concerns is not limited to physical safety concerns.

As engineers, we are problem solvers by nature and training, systems thinking is in our DNA. By focusing on masculinity and mental health in the context of STEM and safety, Mark invites us to use our skills to address the deeper issues which are crucial to safer systems. The pursuit of truly inclusive cultures in our industries is a challenge we must embrace because it will deliver better outcomes for everyone including those who are part of the industry itself.

This book is an important catalyst to stimulate debate. It is also refreshing to see recognition of the need to include everyone including majority groups as well as minorities. Whether you are an engineer, a Health & Safety professional, an educator, or simply a concerned citizen, I believe you will find food for thought and ideas which resonate in *The SAFE Leader: Engineering Inclusive Cultures*.

I commend Mark for his courage and conviction in tackling these significant issues. It is my hope that this book inspires many more of us to feel that we have a role to play in building a more inclusive and mentally healthy culture within our workplaces and beyond.

Dame Judith Hackitt DBE, FREng, FIChemE, FCGI

Dame Judith Hackitt has a long career history in chemicals manufacturing and has always spoke with passion about the importance of Health & Safety. She was Chair of the UK Health & Safety Executive from 2007 to 2016 and chaired the Independent Review of Building Regulations and Fire Safety following the Grenfell Tower tragedy in 2017. She was also Chair of manufacturing trade body Make UK (formerly EEF), a member of the Made Smarter Commission and a Non-Executive Director of the High Value Manufacturing Catapult. She currently chairs Enginuity (the Engineering and manufacturing skills organisation) and is a Non-Executive Director at HS2 Ltd.

An engineer by profession, Dame Judith holds a degree in chemical engineering from Imperial College, London. She is a former Presdient of the Institution of Chemcial Engineers and a Fellow and former Trustee of the Royal Academy of Engineering.

MISSION STATEMENT

❞

Build *physically* and *psychologically* **SAFE** teams and organisations.

– Dr. Mark McBride-Wright, MBE, CEng, MIChemE

The engineering sector lacks diversity and inclusion with many groups underrepresented.

These groups include (but are not limited to) women; ethnic minorities; lesbian, gay, bisexual, trans*, non-binary, queer, and intersex (LGBTQ+); neurodivergent; and people with disabilities.

As such, the engineering sector is missing out on the richness that diverse groups of people bring to a team.

When these groups are given the chance to shine, they increase performance, growth, and innovation whilst improving health, safety, and well-being at the same time.

That's why this book's mission is simple:

> **"To encourage thought leaders, organisations, stakeholders, and shareholders to understand the need for Diversity, Equity, and Inclusion (DEI) and why it's not only the future of business, but also the only sustainable solution in a globalised world."**

I present a new leadership philosophy helping you to become a SAFE Leader©. It is particularly beneficial to people who have been trying to make change within their organisation from a culture perspective, but who perhaps are not getting the desired traction.

Aimed at anyone interested in DEI in business, this book is also a useful tool for practitioners in STEM considering how they can create inclusive cultures using a different method for engaging male-majority teams.

This book is also aimed at students so that they can understand the importance of DEI in STEM – from a cultural perspective, and from a design and engineering perspective.

Readers should use this book to learn how to overcome challenges and barriers when it comes to linking DEI and Health & Safety (H&S) to create a positive organisational culture, both in terms of performance and people.

I hope you enjoy this book and would love to hear from you if it has helped impact your work or thoughts in this area.

Mark

DEDICATION

For my son and daughter, Hunter and Willow.

You help me see the world with the purity of childhood. I hope you both pursue your dreams and be whatever you want to be, with *nothing* holding you back.

Like beautiful butterflies – full of colour, light, and hope. Fly and be free.

Love,

Dada x

ACKNOWLEDGMENTS

This book has been a long time in the making, is a convergence of many themes within my life, and has been influenced by many people. Firstly, thank you to my husband, Sam, who has encouraged me along the way and who has listened to me whenever I have needed it.

Thank you to my family: my Mum, Dad, Ga, and Granddad, whose love and support have been a constant. A special thanks to my in-laws, Annette and Mark, who have provided Sam and I with incredible support with our children, which enables us to pursue our careers. We are especially privileged in this.

From my friends, a special callout to my best friend Cat Ball, who has *always* been there for me since we met at primary school, and who will forever remain someone I look forward to spending time with.

Thank you to Nick Hayward, Hayley and Stuart Montague, and Henriette and Anthony Ofori Berland for all the support you have provided too.

My interest in Diversity, Equity, and Inclusion (DEI) started when I first met Elena Fatisi and Jenny Young from the Royal Academy of Engineering in 2013. I will forever be grateful for your courage in running the event on LGBT in Engineering. This event was a turning point for me, setting me off on a new direction after cofounding InterEngineering.

A special thank-you to John Bradbury. Together through InterEngineering, we have improved the engineering sector for the LGBTQ+ community, and I will miss our get-togethers once you are back in Australia.

Big thank-you as well to the EqualEngineers team: Fayon Dixon, Luigi Bozzo, Christopher Brown, and Elio López Vega, and also our associates Stewart Eyres, Fiona Jackson, and Victor Olisa. Collectively we are doing some transformational stuff, and I am excited for what is yet to come!

Finally, this book is only here because of a lovely, sunny brunch with Jennifer Brown at Lafayette's French Bakery in New York City in November 2021. Jennifer's podcast *The Will to Change* inspired me to shift into DEI consulting. Jennifer kindly introduced me to:

- Erin Weed, who "dug me" to my core finding my passion for "Justice,"
- Eduardo Placer, who has helped me shape my storytelling, and
- Jenn T. Grace and the team at PYP, who have helped create this book.

Thank you to everyone who has played a role in helping me get this to where it is today.

CONTENT WARNING

This book deals with subjects such as suicide, self-harm, homophobia, racism, and prejudice, which some readers may find upsetting. For readers sensitive to these subjects, please take note and proceed with caution.

PREFACE – GUIDANCE NOTES

This book has been written with accessibility in mind, including the sans serif font, chapter clarity, and tone of voice. The chapters are designed to be short, the main points bolded, and literal interpretations offered for any metaphors used. It's written for comprehension and sensitivity and isn't meant to be a long or intimidating read. If you feel you can't read the entire book in one go, here is how you can break down your reading experience.

- **Introduction**
- **Chapter One** explains why the engineering industry needs an operating system upgrade.
- **Chapter Two** explores the history of **physical safety** and its current modernisation.
- **Chapter Three** explores **psychological safety, mental health, and well-being** and their link to DEI.
- **Chapter Four** looks at how **DEI and H&S** support each other through the **Bradley Curve.**
- **Chapter Five** reinvents the **Bradley Curve for psychological safety.**
- **Chapter Six** explores how **DEI and H&S interlink** to create psychological safety.
- **Chapter Seven** offers actionable advice on how to engage the male majority in DEI.
- The **Conclusion** discusses what the future of engineering should look like.

You can either read this book from beginning to end to enjoy the full experience and how each specialism interplays or read individual chapters to guide your learning about the subject of your choice. This is a resource you can come back to as many times as you need.

INTRODUCTION

It's 9:46 a.m., summer 2019, and I am on the coast at a nuclear power station 200 miles outside of London. The air-conditioning is barely working, it's hot, and the room is bright white from the sun reflecting in from outside. I am delivering a training session on inclusive cultures to a team of engineers.

"BZZZZ BZZZZZ, BZZZZZ BZZZZZZ." The plant manager's phone rings. She answers it. Someone has tried to take their life on the power plant site, and she has to go and deal with it. I'm instructed to continue the session, which I acknowledge, and I do.

My stomach feels like jelly. I maintain composure, but inside I am struggling, like a swan who is calm on the surface but is furiously kicking its legs underwater. I don't know what to do.

Somehow, I get to the end of the session. When the plant manager returns, she says that the individual in need of help was, thankfully, rescued and taken to get the support they needed.

Unfortunately, it does not always end up this way.

* * * * * * *

My name is Mark and I am the founder and chief executive of EqualEngineers. We empower organisations to engineer inclusive cultures to attract, develop, and retain talent. I established the business in 2017 to support marginalised communities in engineering and technology. In addition, I am a chartered chemical engineer by background and specialised in safety engineering. I helped businesses create physically safe working environments, making sure that people, plant/machinery, and processes are safe. The ultimate goal is ensuring that the risks from hazards related to physical injuries are minimised to as low as reasonably practicable.

I earned what I call my "rainbow stripes" for Diversity, Equity, and Inclusion (DEI) in engineering when I cofounded the cross-sector network InterEngineering in 2013 to connect, inform, and empower LGBTQ+ engineers and supporters. I grew this organisation to become the largest network in the UK for LGBTQ+ engineers, and we now service this network through EqualEngineers.

One year into my journey as a founder, I discovered the breakdown of suicide rates in the United Kingdom by occupation. The construction, manufacturing, and process industries had the highest suicide rate of all occupations. Statistically, you are more likely to die through suicide working in these industries than from a typical hazard like a dropped object falling from height or electrocution. I did not believe these rates. And so, I decided to do some of our own research and in 2018, EqualEngineers ran our inaugural *Masculinity in Engineering* survey, which received over 800 responses and was open to responses from everyone.

The survey unearthed a mental health crisis: 75 percent of respondents reported mental ill-health, and one in five respondents reported losing a work colleague to suicide. In addition, one in five reported suicidal ideation or self-harm personally. Men were 3.5 times more likely to answer yes to this latter question than women.[1]

One in five
reported suicidal ideation or self-harm personally

We reran the survey in 2021 following the Covid-19 pandemic, asking the same questions. Alarmingly, the number of people reporting suicidal ideation or self-harm *increased* to one in four. This could be due to multiple factors exacerbated by the pandemic. Engineers working on-site on projects which remained operational needed to stay away from home, "bubbling up" with their colleagues for a long time without seeing their loved ones. The lack of familiarity of routine, ambiguity of job uncertainty, and lack of social connection for those who were not in the workplace are just a few examples.

> Self-harm is when you hurt yourself as a way of dealing with very difficult feelings, painful memories, or overwhelming situations and experiences.[2] Suicidal ideation is when you have abstract thoughts about ending your life or feel that people would be better off without you.

---

[1] Mark McBride-Wright, "Masculinity in Engineering Research 2022," EqualEngineers, 2022, https://equalengineers.com/masculinity-in-engineering-report/.
[2] "What Is Self-Harm," Mind, May, 2020, https://www.mind.org.uk/information-support/types-of-mental-health-problems/self-harm/about-self-harm/.

> It can also mean thinking about methods of suicide or making clear plans to take your own life.[3]

> If you are struggling then there is help available. Use QR code at the end of this chapter or the website given to visit a list of places where you can get help.

The intention of inclusion and belonging programmes is to create cultures where you can bring your whole self to work and be your true, authentic self. But it is not working for the male majority, who represent 84 percent of the engineering profession in the UK. Because if it was working, then we would expect lower rates of suicidal ideation and self-harm because people would be able to be open about whatever turbulence is going on in their lives.

The irony is that the toxic masculine culture, which can be so pervasive in male-majority teams, prevents individuals from opening up, from being vulnerable, and from speaking about how they are feeling.

During my years in industry as a practicing safety engineer, I helped organisations create physically safe working environments and cultures. I am now an experienced DEI practitioner, having helped thousands of engineers, delivered training to hundreds of organisations, and researched and authored DEI strategies for many organisations. In this work, I make the case for creating spaces of belonging for historically marginalised communities, and yet something is off.

---

[3] "What Are Suicidal Feelings?" Mind, April, 2020, https://www.mind.org.uk/information-support/types-of-mental-health-problems/suicidal-feelings/about-suicidal-feelings/.

It's an opportunity to be curious about the system that has not historically worked for marginalised communities, but what if in reality it is not safe for the male majority either? The issue is not the male majority . . . the issue is the operating system itself. And as I am a safety engineer at heart, I believe we can solve the problem LIKE AN ENGINEER.

With rigour, we can create a system and sector which works for all.

* * * * * *

I want you to know who you really are, the essence of all the stories and experiences that shaped you – *engineered* you – to become the person you are, at this moment, reading this book. We all have a diversity story, and I want us to explore that.

Some groups have their identity more front-and-centre / in the spotlight than others – especially if they're part of a minoritised community. As a result, this can make people in majority groups feel blamed and shamed for not supporting these groups, and this perceived lack of empathy is most often levied at men.

UK

84% ♂   **88.6%** White

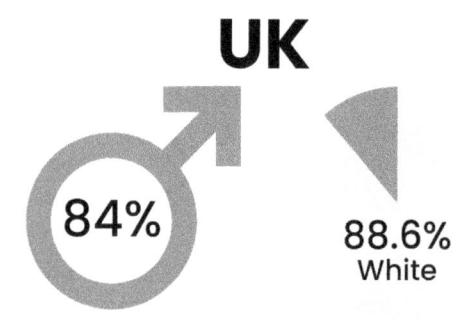

Over 80% male and mostly white.

Figure 0.1. Engineering sector workforce composition in the United Kingdom in terms of sex and ethnicity.

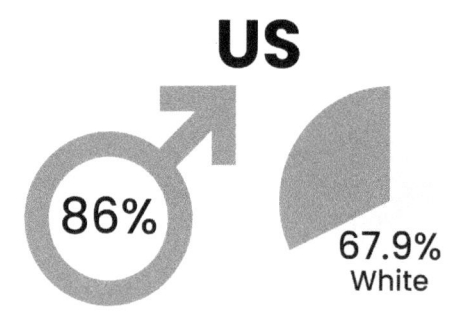

US

86% ♂   **67.9%** White

Over 80% male and mostly white.

Figure 0.2. Engineering sector workforce composition in the United States in terms of sex and ethnicity.

This isn't unfair. In the UK, the engineering sector has a workforce composition of 83.5 percent male in terms of sex, and 88.6 percent white in terms of ethnicity.[4] In the US, it's 86.3 percent male and 67.9 percent white

---

[4] "Trends in the Engineering Workforce between 2010 and 2021," EngineeringUK, https://www.engineeringuk.com/media/318305/trends-in-the-engineering-workforce_engineeringuk_2022.pdf.

INTRODUCTION xxxvii

which means engineering and technology teams are notably made up of cis white males, leading to the "us" and "them" assumptions we're seeking to unravel and resolve.[5] From my experience in delivering training to male-majority groups, most white male engineers do not understand the need for a more representative industry. They perceive DEI programmes as exercises in political correctness and believe their jobs are threatened by the push for representation. Some men feel metaphorically backed into a corner, and so want to lash out against DEI interventions.

For example, it is common when celebrating International Women's Day on 8th March each year, or International Women in Engineering Day on 23rd June each year, to hear "When is it International Men's Day?" (Note: this is on 18th November annually). Or during the Black Lives Matter movement of 2020 to hear "White lives matter too." Or during Pride Month to hear "What about straight pride?"

Many white, cisgendered, heterosexual, neurotypical, nondisabled males who represent the majority feel disenfranchised and alienated in the push for DEI. They feel cancelled and shut down, and the overall tone of social justice feels to me (sometimes) like the villagers with the pitchforks coming to hunt the beasts.

The resultant polarisation hinders change.

People feel like they are walking on eggshells and cannot say anything without fear of offending – it can feel exasperating.

---

[5] "Engineer Demographics and Statistics in the US," Zippia, https://www.zippia.com/engineer-jobs/demographics/.

We need a new way of starting the conversation, and that is what we will explore in this book.

As an industry, engineering underpins everything we encounter daily. It spans sectors such as technology, aerospace, defence, pharmaceutical, renewable energy, manufacturing, construction, oil and gas, medical, healthcare, construction, nuclear, and many others. However, despite its importance, engineering is suffering from a skills shortage. Fewer people are studying Science, Technology, Engineering and Mathematics (STEM) subjects, while the age profile of the engineering workforce is skewed to the upper-age bands.[6] Consequently, the industry is going to lose a significant percentage of skilled workers by 2030 as the workforce retires.

So, what do male-majority teams, skills shortages, and DEI have to do with each other?

It's simple. How they interplay and how they *don't* interplay is the reason the engineering and technology sector is in crisis.

In 2017, suicide was the biggest killer of men aged forty-five and over. The construction, manufacturing, and process industries had the highest rates of male suicide compared to any other industry in the UK, which meant you were statistically more likely to die through suicide than a typical hazard like slips, trips, and falls.

This is alarming and indicates a **mental health emergency in engineering**.

---

[6] EngineeringUK, "Trends in the Engineering Workforce."

Mental health **EMERGENCY** in engineering

The shocking statistics around suicide and self-harm prove we need to do more to help men open up and share how they feel, consequently unleashing the burden of suffering in silence. We need to establish empathy-driven cultures in both our work and home lives and start by understanding our own diversity story – something we all have.

By reviewing the success the engineering industry has achieved in driving down accident rates in terms of physical safety, we're going to explore how this model can be adapted to encompass psychological safety too.

We are going to capitalise on the successful impact of DEI in this area to help support the mental well-being of engineering teams, including the male majority, and create healthier work cultures which are more appealing for new recruits.

We will explore how DEI will play an instrumental part in closing the engineering skills gap and improving psychological safety at work, and we will talk about how to extend this learning to male-majority teams.

CHAPTER ONE

Diversity, Equity, and Inclusion: Foundations and How This Links to Safety in Engineering

What Is Diversity, Equity, and Inclusion?

People often confuse the pursuit of an inclusive culture with achieving a setting where everyone is agreeable with one another. A setting where one group's voice and needs outweighs another's and therefore one group has to give ground for the others to advance. A perception that there is finite opportunity to go around.

Diversity, Equity, and Inclusion (DEI) is actually about allowing conscious difference to coexist such that the sweet spot of innovation can be created. People should expect to be confronted with ideas and expression which they find provoking, offensive, uncomfortable, and even impactful on their core sense of self, as well as ideas and expression with which they agree.

A question to consider is, are we having a dialogue? Or is the "discussion" actually two monologues? A diverse community means a place where a wide diversity of conflicting opinions and ideas exist and are expressed.

Respectful disagreement. Being open to challenge. Two people should be able to disagree with one another, and that is okay.

Indeed, good leadership is where you are prepared to change your mind because you recognise that your experience of the world is different to others. People can sometimes make the mistake of simply arguing their point as opposed to consciously listening to one another.

Dr. Michael Spence, UCL's president and provost, indicates that it is through rigorous and objective exchange, analysis, and challenge that knowledge is expanded. Debates and disagreements foster growth and innovation. The objective is not to "win" but to extend mutual understanding, in which we learn the art of being okay with difference, of strongly disagreeing but still attempting to understand where an opposing view is coming from, of disliking an opinion or idea but not the person holding it.[7]

We need to listen with an open mind and a willingness to genuinely consider alternative viewpoints. This skill of active listening forms part of basic mental health first aid training: listening in to an individual, tuning out the inner monologue in your head, and tuning in to everything which is being said as well as the nonverbal communication, their body language. We also need to suppress the desire to immediately respond because very often that will not mean anything and is simply to make us feel more comfortable. The person may be sharing something with us which is deeply personal and deserves attention.

---

[7] "Provost's Update: How Do We Manage Disagreement and Diverse Views in Our Community?" UCL News, March 22, 2023, https://www.ucl.ac.uk/news/2023/mar/provosts-update-how-do-we-manage-disagreement-and-diverse-views-our-community.

We need to practice finding language which helps foster a culture of increasing understanding. We must never tolerate personal attacks, bullying, or harassment based on a person's identity or their views. This is never excusable, and is something we should advocate against. But we should be able to sit with the uncomfortable sensation that an issue about which we have felt absolutely certain might not be so clear-cut as we thought, that we might even be wrong. This helps us shift from our comfort zone to our thrive zone.

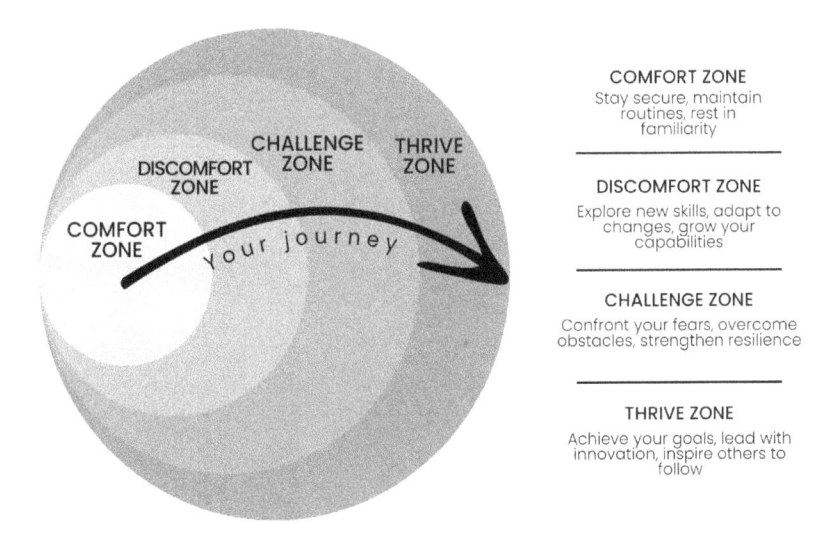

COMFORT ZONE
Stay secure, maintain routines, rest in familiarity

DISCOMFORT ZONE
Explore new skills, adapt to changes, grow your capabilities

CHALLENGE ZONE
Confront your fears, overcome obstacles, strengthen resilience

THRIVE ZONE
Achieve your goals, lead with innovation, inspire others to follow

Figure 1.1. *'Leaving the Comfort Zone'* adaptation, PositivePsychology Toolkit

The Importance of Diversity, Equity, and Inclusion

It's hard to pinpoint the exact moment in time DEI first entered a conversation in the UK. Arguably, the Suffragettes could be considered pioneers of equality while the

Abolition of the Slave Trade Act in February 1807 could be considered a turning point on the road to inclusion.

Diversity is something that has always existed (whether universally acknowledged or not), and the question of when it became a topic of conversation is almost impossible to guess; however, we know the concept of DEI has been in practice for around thirty years.

Because of this fact, the "when" is largely irrelevant. Instead, the questions worth our attention begin with "why?"

- **Why is DEI so important?**
- **Why does DEI require a natural culture shift?**
- **Why is DEI a matter of Health & Safety?**

In this book, we're going to explore the why, and most importantly, the how.

- **How do we embed DEI in our organisations?**
- **How do we ensure every voice is heard and valued?**
- **How do we shift our culture and thinking for both the mental and physical safety of our workforce?**

A common misconception about workplace diversity is that it only references demographics, such as cultural or ethnic differences. It often surprises people when they're told that diversity encompasses a broader spectrum of experiences, including:

- Neurodiversity (aka, cognitive diversity)
- Sex/Gender diversity
- Religious diversity

- Disability diversity
- Sexual orientation diversity
- Age diversity
- Racial diversity

So, when we talk about diversity in this book, we're talking about the rights and values of all these forms.

The world is full of differences, and as we evolve and the age of globalisation brings us and our businesses closer together, the time for widespread DEI is now.

There are some sectors doing their part extraordinarily well, while others have a long way to go on the road to inclusivity.

The focus of this book will be on the engineering industry – a sector embarking on a unique journey as it tries to embed DEI in its various organisations. In doing so, it must tackle toxic masculinity, a mental health crisis, and a skills shortage. There exists similarities across the whole Science, Technology, Engineering, and Mathematics (STEM) sector and so this book can be read with a translatable context.

If that sounds overwhelming, it's not meant to. This book is about sharing uniquely placed insights and expertise, as well as offering guidance and a point of reference on how to implement best practices that *actually* work.

Not only will you be able to make a difference in the lives of your workforce, but you'll also be able to improve your entire organisation's well-being, performance, culture, and safety.

If you are reading this book as an engineering student who will be one of our future leaders, I want you to enter the workforce with empathetic leadership traits as a cornerstone of your practice.

Ethical engineering is now more important than ever before and with this comes the responsibility of ensuring we create an inclusive experience whilst *doing* our engineering, and that this inclusive-centred design flows through to the products and services we engineer.

The premise of this book is to consider an **alternative way to make strides in improving diversity and inclusion within the engineering and technology sector**.

Alternative way to make **strides** in improving **diversity and inclusion** within the engineering and technology sector

We first need to consider how we've been going about having the conversation and evaluate whether we need an alternative approach. Engineering has been operating in an outdated culture mode and needs an upgrade.

> This book will present new and reframed models of engaging with the engineering workforce for creating a cultural transformation in our sector. I will leverage my minoritised identity based on my sexual orientation and historical socioeconomic status whilst also leaning into the privileges I have with being a white, cisgendered, able-bodied male engineer.

DIVERSITY, EQUITY, AND INCLUSION: FOUNDATIONS

For too long, the conversation on inclusivity in engineering has been focused on underrepresented groups, which is having a shallow impact. We are diversifying at a glacial speed in terms of gender and ethnicity and, at our current rates, engineering won't reach gender parity until 2144.[8]

Alarmingly, we are losing women in their thirties to forties, who are leaving the engineering industry due to inability to practise *proper* flexible working. That is, recognising that "flexible working" means more than just part-time. It could mean job-sharing, working from home, compressed hours, flexitime, annualised hours, nine day fortnight, staggered hours, term-time only, phased retirement.

Therefore, it is a basic engineering mass balance that says, "What goes in must come out." If we're losing people from the sector before the end of their careers, we have a problem – especially if we're losing women in this age bracket. At best, we're simply treading water and staying steady. We're not moving, accumulating skills, knowledge, experience, nor wisdom.

The trouble with the conversation around DEI and male-majority teams is how, to date, it's been accusatory, polarising, and divisive when it comes to achieving equity in STEM. The majority feel disenfranchised with constantly being told it's their fault, that they have privilege and therefore should be doing something about it. This has led to an "us and them" culture where the dialogue becomes antidiversity.

For example, in 2023 there has been a sweeping polarisation on LGBTQ issues in the United States in the

---

[8] Jason Arunn Murugesu, "Men Predicted to Outnumber Women in Physics Until the Year 2158," *NewScientist*, January, 11 2023, https://www.newscientist.com/article/2354290-men-predicted-to-outnumber-women-in-physics-until-the-year-2158/.

advertising and business industries. Disney, Target, Bud Light (Anheuser-Busch) are all at the centre of attention when it comes to "us versus them" dialogue, and antidiversity when it comes to public attacks. They are trying to be inclusive and diversify, but not all consumers are open-minded. The fear of losing opportunity is a mentality that has a grip over real change. This also applies in industrial or academic settings, where people in majority groups feel they may have to forego promotional opportunities in order for others to advance.

People are also conflating positive action for positive discrimination.

Positive action: *action to make education, employment, etc. available to members of groups who have traditionally been treated unfairly, for example, because of their race or sex.*[9] *In the US, this is known as affirmative action, despite a highly disputed and unpopular ruling by the Supreme Court.*

Positive discrimination: *the automatic favouring, without proper consideration of merit, of underrepresented individuals from minority groups over individuals in majority groups. Put another way, it refers to the preferential treatment of a group of people over another because they possess a protected characteristic.*[10]

Positive discrimination is illegal under the **UK Equality Act 2010**, but positive action is permissible provided the group it's being applied to has faced historical marginalisation.

---

[9] "Positive Action," Cambridge Online Dictionary, https://dictionary.cambridge.org/us/dictionary/english/positive-action.
[10] "What Is Positive Discrimination?" Davidson Morris, June 25, 2021, https://www.davidsonmorris.com/positive-discrimination/.

Organisations in the UK can take positive action when three conditions are met:[11]

1. You must reasonably think that a group of people who share a protected characteristic and who are, or who could be, using your services:
   a. suffer a disadvantage linked to that characteristic,
   b. have a disproportionately low level of participation in this type of service or activity, or
   c. need different things from this service from other groups.
2. "Reasonably think" means that you can see the disadvantage, low level of participation, or different needs, but you do not have to show any detailed statistical or other evidence. The action you take is intended to:
   - meet the group's different needs,
   - enable or encourage the group to overcome or minimise that disadvantage, or
   - enable or encourage the group to participate in that activity.
3. The action you take is a proportionate way to increase participation, meet different needs, or overcome disadvantages. This means the action is appropriate to that aim and that other action would be less effective in achieving this aim or likely to cause greater disadvantage to other groups.

---

[11] "Equality Act 2010: A Quick Start Guide to Positive Action in Service Provision for Voluntary and Community Organisations," Government Equalities Office, Equality and Diversity Forum, August, 2010, https://assets.publishing.service.gov.uk/government/uploads/system/uploads/attachment_data/file/85026/vcs-positive-action.pdf.

Although positive discrimination is illegal, people often identify an action an organisation is taking as positive discrimination when it's in fact a positive action.

An example could be running a guaranteed interview scheme for people who share their disability status at the point of application to a job opening. This is what they did during the recruitment of the Games' volunteers at the London Olympics 2012. Statistically, it's known that disabled people will not put themselves forward for a role if they don't think they'll be considered. So, the London Olympics' recruiters offered people an interview if they shared at the point of application they had a disability. As a result, they saw an increase in declaration rates; however, everyone still went through the same selection and evaluation process.

What this meant was the London Olympics had more Games Keepers who were openly disabled because there were more in the talent pool. Furthermore, it meant London could run an Olympics that could better cater to **all visitors** making their way around London and the venues. This method was so successful it was adopted by the UK government and now lives on through their "Two Ticks" scheme for Disability Confident employers.[12]

Any positive action has simply sought to create equitable access to participation

---

[12] "Being Disability Confident," UK Government, https://disabilityconfident.campaign.gov.uk/.

It's important to know when to call out the mislabelling of positive action as positive discrimination. The latter perpetuates a perception that a candidate from a minority background has only achieved their participation because of an aspect of their identity, which can be demoralising. Any **positive action has simply sought to create equitable access to participation** because not all people are given the same starting point or have access to the same resources, and talent is available everywhere.

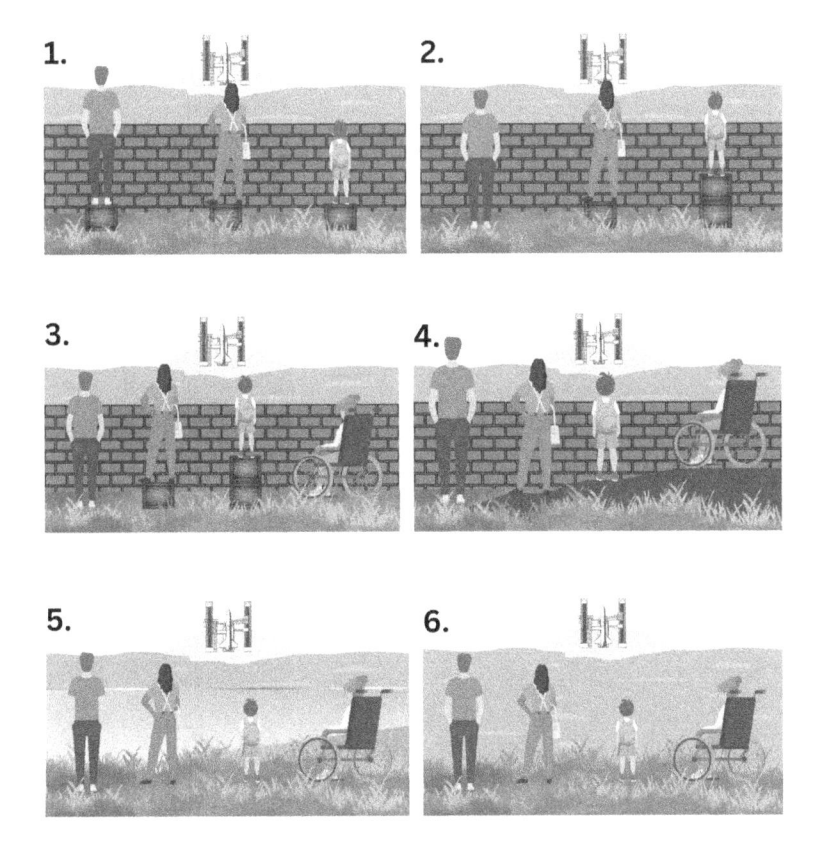

Figure 1.2. '*Illustrating Equality vs Equity*' graphic adaptation, Interaction Institute for Social Change, 2016.

Consider what you see on this image.

In image 1, that is fair, yes? Everyone gets the same intervention. Everyone gets a box. That's fairness. Everyone gets the same. That is equality, no?

In image 2, the shortest person gets two boxes, middle-height person gets one, and the tallest person does not need a box.

Here, we have had an output-driven approach, rather than input-driven. The objective is for everyone to see the shuttle launch. This is achieved in the second image. The privilege in this example is height. We recognise the tallest person is the most privileged and does not need our intervention to participate equally.

People often think with an input-driven mindset, that DEI is about fairness and thus everyone should get the same intervention. This is meaningless in a world where equality of opportunity does not exist. Equity recognises that some people are at a different starting point and so need an intervention in order to participate fairly, thereby levelling the playing field.

Educating your peers on the differences between positive action and positive discrimination can go some way to overcoming negative feelings towards inclusion strategies.

One of these boxes could represent a Returner's Programme. These are permissible because they are giving people the chance to develop leadership/management qualities which they may not have had the privilege of continuous employment to practice because they have had to exit the workforce for some reason (childcare, ill-health, elderly care, etc.). They are getting the chance to acquire these skills to transition back into the workplace.

In image 3, we observe that not all interventions will suit every user. The boxes would not work if a wheelchair user needed support. Therefore we oftentimes have to be creative in our interventions and constantly reviewing their adequacy, relevance, and appropriateness.

In image 4, the use of a ramp means that the opportunity is more accessible for a multiude of heights and mobility requirements. In image 5, we see higher order thinking happening – could we use an alternative material which is transparent such as glass?

We could go back to basics and fundamentally reconsider why there is even a barrier in the first instance. Are we unnecessarily creating inequity for no reason? Do we even need a physical barrier in the first place? We could simply remove the brick wall, as shown in image 6.

This is a form of constant optimisation in engineering design, and this is a skill which engineers should be perfecting and practicing as part of our jobs.

In images 5 and 6, Justice is where all four can see the game without the need for any accommodations or supports because the cause(s) of the inequity was addressed. The systemic barrier has been either removed or adjusted by using risk assessment and design solutions which ensure equitable participation of all, without compromising on safety protections.

Inherent safer design is the practice whereby you design things in such a way that there is a low level of danger even if things go wrong. Inherently Inclusive Design © is the practice of being as broad as practicable in our design stages in giving due considerstion to all stakeholders who will be impacted by our process, product, or service.

Linking Health & Safety with Diversity, Equity, and Inclusion

Throughout this book, I will present a model for engaging with engineers in a new way. Engineers are familiar with physical safety; it's part of our culture and ingrained in us from our initial training and reinforced through the values of the organisations in which we work, including the daily messaging on the projects and teams we're a part of. Going home safe at night to our loved ones is our utmost priority. Being able to call out unsafe acts without fear of retribution is how we work.

Workplace Injuries

In the UK, 565,000 people sustained an injury at work in 2022, according to the UK Labour Force Survey, and 61,713 injuries to employees were reported to the UK Health & Safety Executive (HSE) under Reporting of Injuries, Diseases, and Dangerous Occurrences Regulations (RIDDOR). 36.8 million working days were lost due to work-related illness and workplace injury, at an estimated cost of £18.8 billion.[13]

In the US, about 7.8 million workers missed work in January 2022 because they had an illness, injury, or medical problem or appointment, up from 3.7 million in January 2021.[14]

Workplace incidents, such as dropped objects, falling from height, electrocution, and risks from slips, trips, and

---

[13] "Health & Safety Statistics," Health & Safety Executive, https://www.hse.gov.uk/statistics/.
[14] "7.8 Million Workers Had an Illness-Related Work Absence in January 2022," US Bureau of Labor Statistics, February 9, 2022, https://www.bls.gov/opub/ted/2022/7-8-million-workers-had-an-illness-related-work-absence-in-january-2022.htm.

falls, are all aspects on which time, money, and effort are spent eradicating the associated dangers – or at the very least, minimising them – to as low as reasonably practicable. These efforts aim to make these risks tolerable and are managed on an ongoing basis through risk management processes.

But how are we managing the mental health and well-being of our engineering workforce?

Frankly, we're not, and we need to do better. If the intention of inclusion and belonging programmes is to create a culture where you can bring your whole self to work and be your true, authentic self and not have to mask or hide who you are, then we're delivering these in a vacuum where there's a disconnect with the majority-male workforce.

They're not benefitting from the emotional anchorage that comes with a culture of belonging, as evidenced by the high suicide rates and aversion to openly showing weakness, fear, or emotion (as revealed in the *Masculinity in Engineering* research report).[15] By focusing on the "inclusion" in DEI and welcoming the male majority into that aspect, we're able to create a psychologically safe environment that benefits everyone and improves team performance.

As engineers, we're brilliant at creating *physically* safe work environments and have made tremendous improvements in making our workplaces safer for our physical well-being. So, it's time we do the same for our minds by ensuring we have workplaces free from mental injury, allowing us to create inclusive cultures where *everyone* thrives, including the male majority.

---

[15] McBride-Wright, "Masculinity in Engineering Research."

Key Takeaways

- DEI aims to create a culture where diverse perspectives coexist, leading to innovation through critical and objective exchanges.

- Effective DEI practices require active listening and open-mindedness to different viewpoints, transitioning from one-sided monologues to meaningful dialogues.

- Diversity in DEI extends beyond race and gender to include neurodiversity, religious diversity, and other forms, emphasising the respect for various rights and values.

- There is a key difference between positive action (legal), offering equal opportunities to underrepresented groups, and positive discrimination (illegal), favouring certain groups.

- Engineering must address toxic masculinity, mental health, and skill shortages, while implementing inclusive practices beyond traditional diversity.

- DEI integration in the engineering sector's health and safety protocols is vital, emphasising mental health alongside physical safety.

Scan now and download the resources from this chapter.

Or visit:
equalengineers.com/TheSAFELeader/downloads

CHAPTER TWO

How the Operating System was Built: The History of Physical Safety in Engineering

To understand how far Health & Safety (H&S) standards have already come, we need to look at where we started. The idea of H&S in the workplace is a relatively new concept.

The real beginnings of Health & Safety in the UK were when factory inspectorates were installed in 1833. This was the first real movement towards making people safer in the workplace and helping reduce the number of injuries that were being suffered at the time.[16]

Health & Safety is under continuous improvement around the world. However, it wasn't always a priority for businesses. So, **when was the idea of workplace Health & Safety taken seriously, and how has it progressed since its establishment**?

---

[16] "History of Health & Safety," BCF Group, https://www.thebcfgroup.co.uk/health-and-safety-pages/history-health-safety-workplace.php.

In the past, high injury rates were the norm because there wasn't a concerted effort to manage workplace hazards. Personal Protective Equipment (PPE) was minimal, and the value placed on life was low. Labourers were dispensable, and litigation associated with a loss of life or injury was minimal.

Therefore, people responded to hazards in the workplace based on their inherent built-in tendencies.

Here are the significant dates in history that contributed to current Health & Safety legislation in the UK:[17]

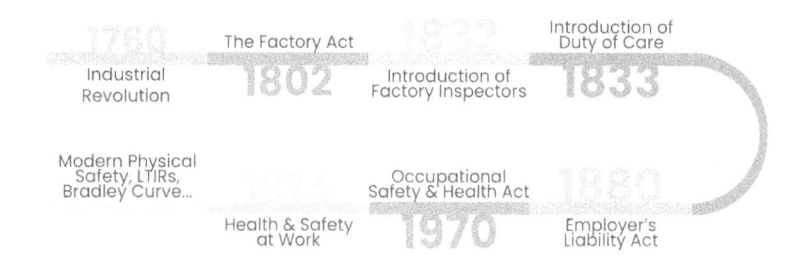

Figure 2.1. The History of Physical Safety in Engineering timeline.

1. Industrial Revolution
2. The Factory Act of 1802
3. Factory Inspectors
4. Duty of Care 1837
5. Employers Liability Act of 1880
6. Occupational Health & Safety Act of 1970
7. Health & Safety at Work Act 1974
8. Bradley Curve 1990

---

[17] Don Cameron, "History of Workplace Health and Safety," StaySafe, https://staysafeapp.com/blog/history-workplace-health-and-safety.

The Industrial Revolution, *1760–1800s*

Before the Industrial Revolution began in 1760, it was the norm to make a living through agriculture or the making and selling of products from home. There were varying levels of protection for workers. While there were some regulations in place, such as those that prevented employers from overworking their employees, these were not particularly stringent and did not provide adequate protection for workers overall.

Britain then began moving towards a society that was fuelled by mass production and the factory system, which prompted the Industrial Revolution. There were pros and cons to the Industrial Revolution. The pros included shifting us from an agrarian economy to a manufacturing economy where products were no longer made solely by hand but by machines. This led to increased production and efficiency, lower prices, more goods, better housing, improvements in transportation networks, improved wages, and migration from rural areas to urban areas.

The Industrial Revolution provided an incentive to increase profits. People moved to cities for work in the new mills and factories; however, the vast number of people looking for work and the need for cheap labour led to poor pay, hazardous factory conditions, and an increase in child labour. Hours were long and conditions dangerous, with loss of life being a common outcome. Unsanitary living conditions, pollution, and food shortages were also common. Health issues arose for many of the factory workers, giving rise to the labor movement throughout the US.[18]

---

[18] Ronni Sandroff, "The History of Unions in the United States," Investopedia, September 1, 2022, https://www.investopedia.com/financial-edge/0113/the-history-of-unions-in-the-united-states.aspx.

The Factory Act, *1802*

The Factory Act of 1802 was a landmark piece of legislation in the history of industrial work in the United Kingdom. It was passed by Parliament in response to increasing public outcry over the dangerous, exploitative working conditions that had become commonplace in many factories and mills throughout England and Wales. The Act gave certain individuals employed at these factories certain rights and protections, including limits on their working hours, a minimum age for employment, and regulations on pay.

Child labour conditions were fought for, which led to the introduction of the **Health and Morals of Apprentices Act of 1802**, commonly known as the **Factory Act**.

The Factory Act required factories to:

- Have windows and openings for ventilation
- Be cleaned at least bi-annually with quicklime and water
- Limit working hours for apprentices to no more than twelve hours a day (excluding time taken for breaks)
- Stop nighttime working by apprentices during the hours of 9:00 p.m. and 6:00 a.m.
- Provide suitable clothing and sleeping accommodation to every apprentice
- Instruct apprentices in reading, writing, arithmetic, and the principles of the Christian religion

The Factory Act sought to improve the lives of those who worked in Britain's new industrial workplaces. On paper, it seemed like a progressive step forward: all workers aged nine or older were restricted from working more than twelve hours per day; children aged between nine and eighteen were limited to eight hours of work a day; and all workers were paid at least six pence per hour.

The Factory Act was also the first UK law to regulate the age of employment in factories. It banned employers from hiring children under nine years old, set the maximum working hours for children between nine and eighteen, and even limited the number of apprenticeships that could be taken on by these young people.

Despite these regulations, however, many employers found ways to circumvent them – paying workers less than the legal minimum wage or extending their working days beyond what was legally allowed. This led to public outcry once again, resulting in further legislation such as the Factory Act Amendment Act of 1844, which tightened regulations around wages and working conditions.

From its inception, the Factory Act of 1802 has been hailed as an important milestone in British industrial history, as it was one of the first pieces of legislation introduced specifically to protect workers' rights and improve their working conditions. Despite being far from perfect – and being regularly circumvented by employers – this law helped set a precedent that eventually led to increased safety and fairness for those employed in Britain's factories and mills.

Although this Act had limited enforcement, the Factory Act is seen as the beginning of Health & Safety regulations.

The Factory Act of 1802 had a lasting impact on employment law not just in Britain but around the world. Its regulations served as a template for similar laws protecting workers' rights throughout Europe, North America, Australia, and beyond. Its introduction also provided more evidence that people could influence their own destinies, and that the government could be a positive force in protecting their interests. The importance of this Act cannot be underestimated, and it stands today as a testament to the power of people and their representatives standing up for those seeking greater safety, fairness, and equity in the workplace.

The Introduction of Factory Inspectors, *1833*

Tired of spending over twelve hours a day in the factories, workers began a movement to reduce working days to ten hours. This was known as the **Ten Hours Movement** championed by MP Anthony Ashley-Cooper and it was fought for after twelve-hour days had become the norm.[19]

TEN HOURS MOVEMENT

The pressure from the tired workers' group led to the Inspectors Act, giving them access to the mills and granting them permission to question workers.

---

[19] "The 1833 Factory Act," UK Parliament, https://www.parliament.uk/about/living-heritage/transformingsociety/livinglearning/19th century/overview/factoryact/.

The Ten Hours Movement was a major social movement of the early 19th century that sought to reduce the working hours of factory labourers in England. The campaign began in 1833, when Parliament passed an Act for regulating factories, commonly known as the Factory Inspectors Act. This Act established the new position of Factory Inspector with the purpose of enforcing a maximum twelve-hour workday for adult workers. The law allowed some exemptions such as workshops producing goods for export and certain types of seasonal businesses.

In response to this legislation, various labour organisations across Britain began organising strikes and protests aimed at reducing their working hours even further. In some cities, demonstrations turned violent and resulted in rioting. Nevertheless, employers slowly began to accept shorter workdays as a way of avoiding strikes. By 1847, the Ten Hours Movement had largely succeeded in its goals and factory workers were working an average of ten hours per day.

The success of the Ten Hours Movement was significant for several reasons. It marked the first time that working conditions had been improved through legislation rather than through collective bargaining between employers and employees. It also demonstrated that labour organisations could effectively organise large-scale social movements to affect meaningful change on behalf of their members. Finally, it showed that government intervention could bring about positive changes in the lives of workers and improve economic efficiency by reducing fatigue-related accidents in factories.

Today, the legacy of the Ten Hours Movement is still felt in Britain's factories and in other places where workers' rights are respected. The movement serves as an important reminder that collective action and government intervention can lead to improvements in working conditions and help ensure a better quality of life for all members of society.

By looking back at this critical juncture in labour history, we can learn valuable lessons about how to advocate for fair working conditions in today's society. The legacy of the Ten Hours Movement shows that when social movements are organised with determination and unified goals, lasting change is possible.

As we strive for better conditions for all workers, let us remember the courageous individuals who organised strikes and demonstrations to make their voices heard more than two centuries ago.

The Introduction of Duty of Care, *1832*

Following an employee's successful compensation claim for work-related injuries caused by their employer, it was established that employers owed employees a **duty of care**.

Duty of Care

A moral or legal obligation to ensure the safety or well-being of others

The concept of "duty of care" was first introduced in 1832 in the English case *Donoghue v Stevenson*.[20] This landmark decision established that people owe a duty of care towards one another, which must be taken into account when assessing civil liability. The court's ruling held that companies were responsible for ensuring their products did not cause harm or injury to their customers and should take reasonable steps to ensure safety.

At the time, the concept of duty of care was relatively new and created much discussion about its implications for businesses and individuals alike. For example, it raised questions about what would constitute an acceptable level of risk for business owners, as well as whether consumers could trust manufacturers to produce safe products.

The ruling also set out a number of principles that must be taken into account when determining whether a duty of care has been breached. These include: foreseeability of risk, proximity between parties, and the reasonable steps that can be taken to mitigate any risks.

The *Donoghue v Stevenson* decision was highly influential in setting the precedent for future rulings on duty of care. From then onwards, many cases have used this ruling as a guide to determine the extent of responsibility owed by businesses towards their customers and other members of society. The concept has since become established in law and is now an important part of tort law, which concerns compensation for harm to people's rights to Health & Safety, a clean environment, property, their economic interests, or their reputations.

---

[20] "Donoghue v Stevenson Case Summary," LawTeacher, December 2, 2023, https://www.lawteacher.net/cases/donoghue-v-stevenson.php.

The introduction of duty of care in 1832 provided individuals with greater protection against harm or injury caused by others, and it continues to do so today. It stands as a reminder of the importance of businesses taking reasonable steps to protect their customers, and it serves as an example of how the law can help ensure that companies remain accountable for their actions. The case has proven to be a landmark decision in legal history, and its implications are still relevant today.

Safety Regulations Increase, *1842–1878*

1842 Mines Act — Graham's Factory Act — **1848** The Locomotive Act — **1878** Factory And Workshop Act
1844 Ten Hour Movement — **1861**

Figure 2.2. Safety Regulations timeline

Over the next thirty-six years, several acts were introduced to protect women and children.

Women and children were prevented from working in underground mines, the use of child labour to clean and maintain moving machinery was stopped, and a fifty-six-hour workweek for women and children was introduced.

The new safety regulations in the UK between 1842 and 1878 were huge steps forward for the working population. After decades of hazardous conditions, these laws sought to improve Health & Safety standards across the country.

One of the key pieces of legislation that was implemented during this time was the Mines Act of 1842, which prohibited children under ten from working in mines. This law also introduced ventilation systems and improved access for medical care if miners were injured on the job.

In addition, the Factory Acts of 1844–1878 regulated work hours, including limiting them to no more than ten hours per day for children under sixteen. It also set limits on how many hours women could work each day.

In 1847 and 1848, the work week was adjusted to fifty-eight hours so that women and children could work for twelve hours. With the Ten Hour Movement in 1848, the working hours were shortened to ten hours per day (from 5:30 a.m. to 8:30 p.m.) for women and children under the age of eighteen.

In 1850 that would change to 6:00 a.m. to 6:00 p.m. or 7:00 a.m. to 7:00 pm., depending on the season, making it a sixty-hour work week.

In 1878 the Factory and Workshop Act, the ban on Sunday working (and on late working on Saturday), was modified to apply instead to the Jewish Sabbath where both employer and employees were Jewish. Through these legislations, workers were given necessary breaks during the day, and their working environment was made safer.

The Locomotive Act of 1861 regulated the speed at which trains could travel as well as stipulating that all train drivers must be sober while driving. This act was seen by many as a major accomplishment in terms of regulating transportation safety standards.

Several trade unions were set up in order to help create better working conditions for labourers. They worked towards ensuring fair wages and later limiting lead paint or asbestos. Overall, these regulations, unions, and other initiatives helped to create a much safer working environment for labourers in the UK.

These regulations were not without their critics, however. Some argued that the laws were too restrictive and would limit the overall productivity of British industry. Proponents of these safety measures, on the other hand, argued that in order to protect workers from exploitation and dangerous working environments, regulation was necessary.

The debate over safety regulations continues to this day, with many companies and countries struggling to find a balance between protecting employees from potential harm, whilst allowing for maximum efficiency and production. UK Safety Regulations between 1842–1878 were extremely influential on global Health & Safety standards and paved the way for future legislation.

The Health & Safety Executive (HSE) formed in 1975 in order to monitor and enforce Health & Safety regulations across the UK. These laws set a precedent for workplace safety all over the world, ensuring that workers are provided with healthy and safe working conditions.

Today the UK is considered one of the safest countries in the world for workers due to its extensive safety regulations. It has often been credited as a pioneer in workplace safety law and continues to set an example for other countries around the globe. As a result of these laws, millions of people all over the world are now able to work in a safe and healthy environment.

The Employer's Liability Act, *1880*

Following the establishment of duty of care from *Donoghue v Stevenson* in 1832, the **Employer's Liability Act** enabled all workers to seek compensation for injuries resulting from the negligence of an employer.

The Employer's Liability Act of 1880 was a landmark piece of legislation which reshaped how employers interacted with their workers and held them accountable for workplace safety. It provided a framework for employees to receive justice when they were subjected to harm or injury due to their employer's negligence.

In order for an employee to succeed in bringing a claim against their employer, the statute specifies that the injury must have occurred due to the negligence of the employer. Negligence is defined as failing to take reasonable precautions against foreseeable risks or hazards. The Act outlines specific requirements that employers must meet in order to protect their employees and avoid potential liability claims. These include providing safe equipment and machinery, proper ventilation, adequate lighting, appropriate training, and regular maintenance of work premises.

The Act meant any worker or their family was entitled to compensation for injury or death. This was on the condition it was caused by a defect in equipment or machinery, or negligence of a person given authority over the worker by the employer.

It imposed increased responsibilities on employers to ensure that their employees had safe conditions and adequate protection from accidents, injury, or disease due to the workplace environment. The Act also provided a framework for employees who were harmed by their employer's negligence to seek compensation from them.

The Act marked a significant shift away from previous laissez-faire approaches which relied on individuals using common law remedies. From this point onward, it became obligatory for employers to take responsibility for their workers' safety and welfare. The Act applies to all kinds of workplaces, including factories, mines, construction sites, and fields where manual labour is carried out.

In order to ensure compliance with the terms of the Act, employers must take reasonable steps to reduce risks and hazards in their workplace. This includes implementing Health & Safety policies which are regularly updated, providing employees with relevant training, and ensuring that these policies are enforced by proper supervision and monitoring.

If employers fail to meet these standards, they may be held liable for any injury or illness suffered by employees due to their negligence. Furthermore, if an employer is found guilty of inadequate safety measures which led to employee injury or death, they face significant fines or even imprisonment as a punishment.

The Employer's Liability Act of 1880 has provided important protections for employees and helped to shape the modern workplace. It is crucial that employers take their legal requirements seriously, as failure to do so can lead to serious consequences. By taking appropriate steps to comply with the terms of the Act, employers can ensure that their workers are provided with adequate protection from harm and injury in the workplace.

The Employer's Liability Act of 1880 remains an integral part of British law today and serves as a reminder of how vital it is for employers to provide safe conditions for their employees. It is therefore essential that all businesses make sure they understand and adhere to the terms of this important piece of legislation.

A Continued Increase in Acts and Reforms, *1880–1970s*

Health & Safety continued to flourish over the period of a century with a focus on safeguarding machinery and raising the legal working age. As a result, more workplace inspectors were appointed across industries.

In 1906, the Workmen's Compensation Act was passed, granting compensation to any worker injured as a result of their work. This Act also established an independent body, the National Insurance Commission (NIC), to oversee all insurance claims related to workplace injuries.

In 1911, the National Health Insurance Act was passed, establishing a contributory insurance scheme and providing financial support to those unable to work owing to illness or disability.

1947 saw the National Health Service (NHS), providing free healthcare access to all citizens.

Further reforms were introduced through the Health & Safety at Work Act 1974, introducing a new system for enforcing workplace Health & Safety standards across all UK businesses. This was followed by the passing of the Safety Representatives and Safety Committees Act in 1977, granting workers the right to elect safety representatives and inspect their workplaces for any potential hazards.

The continuous series of Acts and reforms passed between 1880 and the 1970s have ensured that workers in the UK are provided with safe and healthy working conditions. These Acts have also helped to reduce the risk of workplace accidents, illnesses, and fatalities, ensuring that employees can work without fear of harm or injury.

In addition, they have improved employee morale by giving employees more rights and protection when it comes to their Health & Safety. As a result of these efforts, the number of workplace-related incidents has dropped significantly over recent decades. The UK continues to strive for further improvement in Health & Safety standards as technology advances.

This is an ongoing effort which will ensure a safe and healthy working environment for generations to come.

Occupational Safety and Health Act (United States), *1970*

The main goal of the Occupational Safety and Health Act of 1970 was to ensure all employers provided employees with a work environment free from hazards, including exposure to toxic chemicals, excessive noise levels, mechanical dangers, heat or cold stress, and unsanitary conditions.

The Occupational Safety and Health Act was passed by Congress on December 29, 1970, to ensure safe and healthy working conditions for workers in the United States. The law created the Occupational Safety and Health Administration (OSHA) within the Department of Labor with a mission to prevent workplace injuries, illnesses, and deaths through enforcement of standards in safety and health regulations.

The Act also led to the creation of the **National Institute for Occupational Safety and Health** (NIOSH). NIOSH is a research and education institution, not a legal enforcement agency. While OSHA creates and enforces regulations, NIOSH focuses its attention on pushing the scientific field of occupational safety forward. They share the results of their research through robust education programs.

In addition to creating OSHA, the Act also authorised states to create their own occupational safety programs if they met or exceeded federal standards. Currently, twenty-nine states have state-run occupational safety and health plans that are approved by the US Department of Labor.[21]

The Occupational Safety and Health Act requires employers to provide employees with information about hazardous materials and safety procedures in the workplace, to train employees in safety practices, and to develop a comprehensive safety program. Employers must also keep records of illnesses and injuries that occurred in their workplaces and report any fatalities to OSHA.

The Act has been amended four times since its original passage, most recently in 1992. These amendments have expanded OSHA's authority so it can enforce standards more strictly, increase fines for violations of these standards, improve whistleblower protections against employers who retaliate against workers filing complaints with OSHA, and establish the Voluntary Protection Programs (VPPs) which reward low-risk worksites with reduced inspections.

---

[21] "State Plans," Occupational Safety and Health Administration, US Department of Labor, https://www.osha.gov/stateplans/.

Since its inception, the Occupational Safety and Health Act has resulted in dramatic reductions of accidents and deaths in the workplace. The number of fatalities and injuries has decreased by more than 60 percent since 1970, and OSHA estimates that compliance with its standards prevents more than 4 million workplace illnesses and injuries every year. The Occupational Safety and Health Act has made a significant impact on the safety of workers in the United States.

The success of the Occupational Safety and Health Act can be credited to its strict enforcement of standards. In addition to developing regulations for employers to follow, OSHA also carries out regular inspections of worksites across the country, focused on protecting worker Health & Safety. If an employer is found to be in violation of any regulations or standards, they can face civil penalties or even criminal prosecution. Employers who are found to be in violation of the Act can also be required to take corrective action, such as providing appropriate safety training or equipment.

OSHA has made it clear that protecting worker Health & Safety is their top priority. Their efforts have helped improve conditions for millions of American workers, making life safer and healthier for generations to come. By upholding the standards set forth in the Occupational Safety and Health Act, employers can ensure a safe work environment for their employees and help create a more productive workforce.

With its commitment to protecting employee well-being, the Occupational Safety and Health Act continues to serve as an important tool in keeping workers safe from harm each day. As we look forward into the future, it is likely that OSHA will continue to make safety a priority and work to ensure that all working conditions are safe and healthy for everyone.

Health & Safety at Work Act, *1974*

The **Health & Safety at Work Act 1974** was a revolutionary piece of legislation that forms the basis of Health & Safety legislation across the world today.

The Act is a cornerstone of UK law, providing the framework for workplace Health & Safety across all industries. Under the Act, employers are required to protect the health, safety, and welfare of their employees while they are at work. This includes taking reasonable measures to reduce risks from dangerous machinery, hazardous materials, and working conditions.

Employers must also provide appropriate training and information on Health & Safety matters, as well as ensure that adequate facilities such as toilets, rest areas, first aid equipment, and hazard warning signs are provided. Additionally, workers have an obligation to take reasonable care for their own safety in accordance with their employer's instructions.

In order to enforce these regulations effectively, the Act established the UK **Health & Safety Executive (HSE)** as an independent body to promote and enforce Health & Safety legislation. It is also responsible for approving codes of practice that are relevant to each industry, as well as publishing guidance on how employers can comply with the Act. In addition, local authorities have the power to enforce regulations through unannounced inspections and other enforcement activities.

Overall, the Act provides a comprehensive framework of regulations designed to protect workers in all industries across the UK. By observing these rules, employers can ensure that their employees stay safe while they are at work. Additionally, complying with this legislation will help organisations to avoid costly fines or legal action that could arise from any failure to observe Health & Safety standards.

The Act is an important part of the UK law and a vital piece of legislation for ensuring the safety of workers in all industries. Employers must ensure that their organisations are compliant with all relevant regulations to protect their employees from harm and prevent costly consequences. Through observing Health & Safety protocols, employers can create a safe working environment where staff feel protected, respected, and valued.

Unlike previous Acts in the UK, the Health & Safety at Work Act encompasses all industries and employees. The Act places responsibility on both the employer and employee. Under Health & Safety law, the primary responsibility for this comes down to employers. Workers also have a duty to take care of their own Health & Safety and that of others who may be affected by their actions at work. Workers must cooperate with employers and coworkers to help everyone meet their legal requirements.[22] This is to ensure the health, safety, and well-being of individuals across all workplaces and members of the public who could be affected by work activities.

As a result of the Act, there was a 73 percent reduction in the number of workplace fatalities over the next forty years, and nonfatal injuries also fell by 70 percent.

---

[22] "Lone Workers," Health & Safety Executive, https://www.hse.gov.uk/lone-working/worker/.

2010s and Beyond

The **Health & Safety at Work Act 1974** still forms the basis of workplace safety law in the UK, and it influenced legislation in Europe, New Zealand, and other parts of the world.

While the principles have remained the same, the Act continues to evolve. Updates and reforms are continually reviewed as workplaces go through evolutions, bringing new Health & Safety challenges to the fore.

Modern Physical Safety

Engineering involves working in environments where accidents can happen, and the potential for major injury or a large loss of life exists. This is because the **industries engineers work in are often considered high-risk**. For example, construction and industrial engineers work with heavy machinery that can break and cause injury; chemical engineers deal with toxic or noxious materials that can easily lead to health concerns if not properly handled; and civil engineers are at risk on work sites, due to trips, slips, and falls from heights.

Lost Time Incident Rates (LTIRs)

Industries such as construction, oil and gas, pharmaceuticals, rail, nuclear, defence, and marine are just some of the many industries employing engineering professionals where preserving life is a core tenet of the culture of the organisation. Each industry has a relevant regulator who ensures safety standards are maintained and issues licences to operate (where relevant). Audits are carried out on predefined and ad-hoc bases.

The metric tracked is **Lost Time Incident Rates** (LTIRs). A lost time accident is an incident that has resulted in an employee needing to miss work due to sustaining an injury while working (only accidents that happen "on the clock" are considered in this metric).

The OSHA Form 300 is a form for employers to record all reportable injuries and illnesses that occur in the workplace, where and when they occur, the nature of the case, the name and job title of the employee injured or made sick, and the number of days away from work or on restricted or light duty, if any.

OSHA defines the criteria for recordable injuries and illnesses as:[23]

> "Death, days away from work, restricted work or transfer to another job, medical treatment beyond first aid, or loss of consciousness."

The higher the incident rate, the lower your organisation's safety performance. Since this metric is calculated in hindsight, it isn't a perfect predictor of an organisation's future safety performance. However, it's still important to track because it allows for the opportunity to prevent similar incidents from happening again in the future.

Some organisations deploy a percentage of executive pay linked to a continuous reduction in LTIRs. Hence the reason it's tracked, scrutinised, and reported on. If there is any increase, then the executives will forego this share of their remuneration. It's a classic example of "what gets measured and monitored gets done." It also highlights

---

[23] "Recording and Reporting of Occupational Injuries and Illnesses," Occupational Safety and Health Administration, https://www.osha.gov/laws-regs/regulations/standardnumber/1904/1904.7.

why there is so much investment in safety culture programmes and the adoption of schemes such as the Stop Work Authority cards (mentioned later).

The Bradley Curve

The Bradley Curve, developed by DuPont in the 1990s, is a critical tool used in safety engineering to measure risk. The Bradley Curve shows how safety systems must be designed to protect people from catastrophic events. The curve illustrates that as the culture improves, the probability of an incident occurring decreases exponentially.

At each point on the curve, there are two components: hazard exposure time and risk of harm. As hazard exposure time increases, so does the risk of harm; however, at some point along the curve, additional exposure time no longer increases the likelihood of an accident or injury occurring. This point marks what is known as a "safety limit" – after which additional risks are negligible.

The Bradley Curve serves as a helpful tool to guide safety engineers in their decisions on what systems should be designed and implemented. By understanding the Bradley Curve, engineers can determine which safety systems will provide optimal protection against hazardous events with minimal cost or effort. Additionally, it can help predict how safe a system will be over time, allowing for proactive measures to be taken before an incident occurs.

Today, the Bradley Curve remains one of the most influential tools used by safety engineers when designing and managing complex safety systems. It helps ensure that all components of a system are working together efficiently and safely and highlights areas where improvements can be made. The Bradley Curve is an essential part of modern engineering practice, and its development has helped save countless lives. We will introduce this useful tool in Chapter 5 and explore how we can apply it.

Organisational Responsibility

The **Health & Safety at Work Act 1974**, which became a flagship piece of UK legislation, brought together lots of disparate pieces of past legislation under one umbrella, making it clear that the responsibility of ensuring workplace safety rights rests with employers.

It opted for a goal-based regime, whereby an organisation needs to quantify hazards based on their probability of happening and their severity of impact were they to happen (i.e., could they result in minor injuries, major injuries, or loss of life?). An organisation then needs to define what measures are put in place to reduce this risk to as low as reasonably practicable (ALARP). A goal-based regime outlines the standard that needs to be achieved and then leaves it up to an organisation to demonstrate *how* it will be achieved.

The United States OSHA has a slightly different approach, which is more prescriptive. It includes a defined list of actions identifying what an organisation *must* do. The upside of a prescriptive regime is that it offers an element of confidence to an organisation so they know they've covered everything needed to obtain regulatory approval. **The downside is that it can drive a box-ticking mentality and a false sense of security** that assumes: if you've done everything listed, you'll be safe. In reality, safety management is all about **managing risk**, meaning there will always be an element of **residual risk**.

Therefore, a blended approach is beneficial. Commonly agreed-on approaches through industry collaboration showcasing good practices are shared for commonplace hazards, and then a heightened awareness is maintained for managing residual risk.

Stop Work Authority Cards

Figure 2.3: Example of Stop Work Authority cards

Stop Work Authority cards are given to employees to remind them that they have the authority and responsibility to stop work if they identify any unsafe actions or hazards that could endanger themselves or others. They present a process to:

1. Stop the activity/behaviour
2. Notify the person in charge (e.g., supervisor to address the issue)

3. Involve the right people (discuss concerns / correct the issue)
4. Resume work
5. Share lessons learned (i.e., potentially impacted employees and contractors)

Carrying Stop Work Authority cards with us at all times on site gives us a passport to intervene when we see something unsafe or unjust happening, irrespective of whether you're the site leader or a recently joined apprentice. Independent of hierarchy, we have a flat structure where all voices matter when it comes to being constantly vigilant for anything that could lead to a lost time incident rate, minor injuries, major injuries, or, at its worst, single and/or multiple fatalities.

There is a risk our **Stop Work** card approach is intrinsically flawed

There is a risk our Stop Work card approach is intrinsically flawed. People might not feel safe bringing up their safety concerns if the person they see violating safety regulations is a superior or they're from a minoritised community (e.g., if a woman observes a group of men violating the safety standards or a person of colour observes a white person violating them).

Our entire Health & Safety reporting system may be fundamentally flawed due to a historical lack of representation and the absence of underrepresented groups from its development. This supports the argument for creating inclusive cultures for improving the systems and processes we use today.

Stop Work Authority only addresses one of the factors that inhibit people from speaking up – the fear of formal punishment for insubordination or slowing productivity. The Bystander Effect has shown that the more people there are around, the less likely we are to speak up.[24] Even in an emergency medical situation, the Bystander Effect is very problematic. You cannot assume someone will call emergency services when someone is in cardiac arrest.

Identifying the Difference Between Hazard Types

The management of risk against hazards requires the constant vigilance of the workforce in a high-risk environment. At this point, it's worth demarcating the difference between process/technical safety hazards and occupational Health & Safety hazards.

> **Process/technical safety hazards** pertain to risks associated with running a plant or an engineered system, which by virtue of its operation has the potential to cause harm if something goes wrong. For example, a leak from a high-pressure gas line could lead to an explosion, resulting in loss of life; a train travelling at speed could derail, which could lead to a loss of life; a captain manoeuvring a large tanker in a shallow marina to connect to a jetty could misjudge distance

---

[24] Rohit Talwar, "STOP Cards Are Not Working! Why?" LinkedIn post, January, 2021, https://www.linkedin.com/pulse/stop-cards-working-why-rohit-talwar.

> and impact the jetty, resulting in damage to facilities and physical injuries.
>
> **Occupational Health & Safety hazards** result from working in an environment with common hazards, which could result in physical injury. For example, walking around without a lid on a hot drink could result in a burn if a person were to collide, slip, trip or fall, or walking up or down the stairs without holding a handrail could lead to a trip or fall, resulting in minor or major injury.

Most engineering businesses have safety programmes that seek to minimise loss of life and foster an internal culture of **calling out any unsafe acts without fear of retribution**. They come under different names or guises such as "Target Zero" or "Zero Harm," but essentially all have the same common goal – to make sure people go home safe and uninjured after performing their workplace tasks. Preserving life is a core tenet of the culture of engineering organisations; however, this has yet to be explicitly extended to the loss of life from suicide.

I have worked in businesses where, if you ever saw any action being performed that put someone's physical safety at risk, challenging and calling out these unsafe acts was actively encouraged.

This may sound obvious – and one would assume innate human nature means we'd intervene without thought – but hierarchical power structures have a strong influence on how people behave, even in fight-or-flight situations. This is why engineering has adopted such a strong and constant approach to safety management, embedding it as part of its core culture to overcome the tendency for people to stay silent.

Current legislation drives an H&S box-ticking mentality, and hierarchical power structures make it hard for some people – especially those with underrepresented characteristics – to speak out. To change these power structures, we need to make calling out unsafe acts something everyone can do without fear of retribution. This is where DEI and inclusive H&S can work together to create psychological safety, making it possible for everyone in a workplace to feel empowered to speak up.

How can we adapt this system and utilise it for our benefit in engineering inclusive cultures? This is something we will now go on to explore.

Key Takeaways

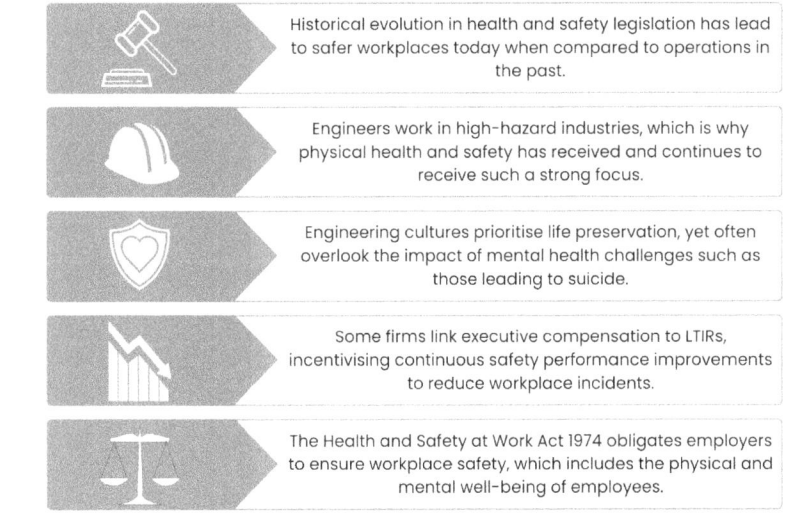

- Historical evolution in health and safety legislation has lead to safer workplaces today when compared to operations in the past.

- Engineers work in high-hazard industries, which is why physical health and safety has received and continues to receive such a strong focus.

- Engineering cultures prioritise life preservation, yet often overlook the impact of mental health challenges such as those leading to suicide.

- Some firms link executive compensation to LTIRs, incentivising continuous safety performance improvements to reduce workplace incidents.

- The Health and Safety at Work Act 1974 obligates employers to ensure workplace safety, which includes the physical and mental well-being of employees.

Scan now and download the resources from this chapter.

Or visit:
equalengineers.com/TheSAFELeader/downloads

CHAPTER THREE

SOS:
The Failure of the Current Safety Operating System

Engineering needs an upgrade. Our present-day culture is operating in a system that is becoming obsolete. A culture that's moving into the past. We are operating in the late-majority/laggards section of our willingness to adopt innovative approaches to changing our culture. This has to change.

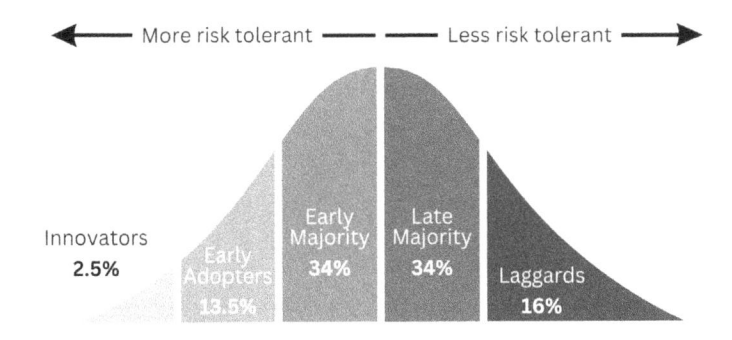

Figure 3.1. *Adopter categorisation on the basis of innovativeness*[25].

---

[25] Michael Mullany, "The Power of the Adoption Curve," LinkedIn post, April 18, 2018, https://www.linkedin.com/pulse/basics-adoption-curve-michael-mullany/.

If I consider Microsoft, who dominated the PC market with the Windows PC in the 90s and early 2000s, I grew up in a world where the "blue screen of death" meant I had to reboot my computer because my machine had picked up a virus. As a result, antivirus software upgrades were a necessity to protect me from any nasties my PC could contract while browsing the internet.

The rise of Apple in the early '00s with their "think different" slogan saw me switch my allegiance from Microsoft to MacBooks (hence the growth in the iOS Operating System). Consumers no longer required an active anti-virus software installation because it was implicit within MacBooks' protection systems, their headaches with Microsoft were eradicated, and their loyalty to Apple was cemented.

So, based on this evolution of technology, a question for consideration is**: Are we fundamentally trying to reshape an integral sector using an Operating System that's inefficient, difficult to use, prone to breaking down, and no longer fit-for-purpose?**

The answer is *yes*, and we need a new way.

Covid-19's Impact on the Engineering Workforce

In March 2020, the global economy shut down and went into hibernation whilst we fought the onslaught of the Coronavirus-19 infection. Global economies were affected and industries such as aerospace were closed, travel was restricted, and a new way of life was thrust upon us with lockdown measures.

FAILURE OF THE CURRENT SAFETY OPERATING SYSTEM 49

Companies that were already investing time and money in moving their workforce to remote and digital operations were able to act with agility and pivot to a 100 percent remote setup with minimal impact. These organisations were the early adopters of truly flexible working policies.

Organisations who'd fought against such a transition or met requests for remote/flexible working with a wrinkled nose found themselves having to scramble. They needed to make sure their IT provisions supported their workers to work from home, then order equipment, have it security checked, validated, and then mailed to their employees. As a result, demand for online platforms such as video conferencing skyrocketed. Who doesn't know the joys of Zoom or Teams nowadays?

In terms of attitudes to remote/flexible working, it took a physical virus to force a full-blown Operating System reset. This was now the only option for the knowledge economy, and organisations had to embrace it or face a cessation of operations.

Engineers were considered key workers during the pandemic – especially those working on critical infrastructure and even on projects that couldn't afford to become behind schedule. This meant that new rules needed to be adopted for working on site, meaning more isolation from colleagues but an increased risk of being exposed to Covid-19 due to the nature of their roles. They were forced to work or risk losing their jobs when others could safely quarantine at home.

Shift patterns of time-on-time-off were stopped, and some engineers went months without seeing loved ones because they were not "bubbled up" with their family – just a subset of colleagues instead. As a result, mental health suffered, as reported in the 2022 *Masculinity in Engineering* report.[26]

Now the sector has gone through a pandemic and forced operational shift, we're better equipped to physically respond should it ever occur again. However, in terms of supporting engineers' mental health, we still have a long way to go when it comes to resetting the Operating System.

Case Study

I discovered the following gem of a case study when researching masculinity in engineering. It covers the story of a culture change programme deployed across two offshore oil platforms in the Gulf of Mexico. These platforms had majority-male workforces, and their leadership styles were characterised by fear, power, dominance, and control.

Ely and Meyerson performed a landmark piece of fieldwork which they report in their 2010 paper "Unmasking Manly Men."[27] This case study of two offshore oil platforms illustrates how an organisational initiative designed to enhance safety and effectiveness created a culture that unintentionally released men from societal imperatives for "manly" behaviour, prompting them to let go of masculine-image concerns and to behave instead in counter-stereotypical ways.

---

[26] McBride-Wright, "Masculinity in Engineering Research."
[27] Robin J. Ely and Debra E. Meyerson, "Unmasking Manly Men: The Organizational Reconstruction of Men's Identity," Academy of Management, November 30, 2017 https://doi.org/10.5465/ambpp.2006.27161322.

Case Study: Unmasking Manly Men

What can managers in white-collar firms learn from roughnecks and roustabouts on an offshore oil rig? That extinguishing macho behaviour is vital to achieving top performance. That's a key finding from a study of life on two oil platforms, during which we spent several weeks over the course of nineteen months living, eating, and working alongside crews offshore.

Oil rigs are dirty, dangerous, and demanding workplaces that have traditionally encouraged displays of masculine strength, daring, and technical prowess. But over the past fifteen years or so, the platforms we studied have deliberately jettisoned their hard-driving, macho cultures in favour of an environment in which men admit when they've made mistakes and explore how anxiety, stress, or lack of experience may have caused them; appreciate one another publicly; and routinely ask for and offer help. These workers shifted their focus from proving their masculinity to larger, more compelling goals: maximizing the safety and well-being of coworkers and doing their jobs effectively.

The shift required a new attitude toward work, which was pushed from the top down. If you can't expose errors and learn from them, management's thinking went, you can't be safe or effective. Workers came to appreciate that to improve safety and performance in a potentially deadly environment, they had to be open to new information that challenged their assumptions, and they had to acknowledge when they were wrong.

Their altered stance revealed two things: First, that much of their macho behaviour was not only unnecessary but actually got in the way of doing their jobs, and second, that their notions about what constituted strong leadership needed to change. They discovered that the people who used to rise to the top – the "biggest, baddest roughnecks," as one worker described them – weren't necessarily the best at improving safety and effectiveness. Rather, the ones who excelled were mission-driven guys who cared about their fellow workers, were good listeners, and were willing to learn.

Over a fifteen-year period these changes in work practices, norms, perceptions, and behaviours were implemented company-wide. The company's accident rate declined by 84 percent, while productivity (number of barrels produced), efficiency (cost per barrel), and reliability (production "up" time) increased beyond the industry's previous benchmark.

But the changes had an unintended effect as well. The men's willingness to risk a blow to their image – by, for example, exposing their incompetence or weakness when necessary in order to do their jobs well – profoundly influenced their sense of who they were and could be as men. No longer focused on affirming their masculinity, they felt able to behave in ways that conventional masculine norms would have precluded.

If men in the hypermasculine environment of oil rigs can let go of the macho ideal and improve their performance, then men in corporate America might be able to do likewise. Numerous studies have examined the costs of macho displays in contexts ranging from aeronautics to manufacturing to high tech to the law. They show that men's attempts to prove their masculinity interfere with the training of recruits; compromise decision quality; marginalize women workers; lead to civil and human rights violations; and alienate men from their health, feelings, and relationships with others. The price of men's striving to demonstrate their masculinity is high, and both individuals and organisations pay it.

The problem lies not in traditionally masculine attributes per se – many tasks require aggressiveness, strength, or emotional detachment – but in men's efforts to prove themselves on these dimensions, whether in the hazardous setting of an offshore oil platform or in the posh, protected surroundings of the executive suite. By creating conditions that focus people on the real requirements of the job, rather than on stereotypical images believed to equate with competence, organizations can free employees to do their best work.

Rather than proving how tough, proficient, and cool-headed they were, as was typical of men in other dangerous workplaces, platform workers readily acknowledged their physical limitations, publicly admitted their mistakes, and openly attended to their own and others' feelings.

Importantly, platform workers did not replace a conventional image of masculinity with an unconventional one and then set out to prove the new image – revealing mistakes strategically, for example, or competing in displays of sensitivity. Instead, the goal of proving one's masculine credentials, conventional or otherwise, appeared to no longer hold sway in men's workplace interactions.

It was reading the work of Ely and Meyerson which made me think this is an opportunity to transform the engineering industry everywhere. Being able to challenge the fundamental constructs of a highly masculine culture, and to create empathy, vulnerability, and replace leadership through fear, power, and dominance with curiosity, compassion, and inclusivity is the end goal.

Much of this is intrinsically linked to psychological safety, and in many cases we already have a workforce whereby the construct of safety is part of the core culture, the fabric of what it means to work in a high-risk industry. Surely, therefore, it would not be too much of an extrapolation to leverage this for achieving a transformation at scale which this study shows can be possible?

What if *every* engineering site and asset in the world had such an intervention? What if every industry with high hazard potential and risks, every organisation that has safety as a core tenet, adopted a similar intervention? Oil and gas, nuclear, rail, defence, construction, pharmaceuticals, manufacturing, maritime, aviation, aerospace, and many more . . . there exists a very significant, scalable potential here.

This is an open invitation to any leader, manager or engineer working in high-hazard industries to join our Project SHIELD©.

- Safety
- Health
- Inclusion
- Equity
- Learning
- Development

We are cocreating a new way to expedite rapid culture change in a meaningful, transformative way. Visit the link via the QR code at the end of this chapter for more information.

FAILURE OF THE CURRENT SAFETY OPERATING SYSTEM   55

Safety
Health
Inclusion
Equity
Learning
Development

Figure 3.2. Project SHIELD© description graphic.

Trusting Teams

Trusted 10 Exercise
Part 1

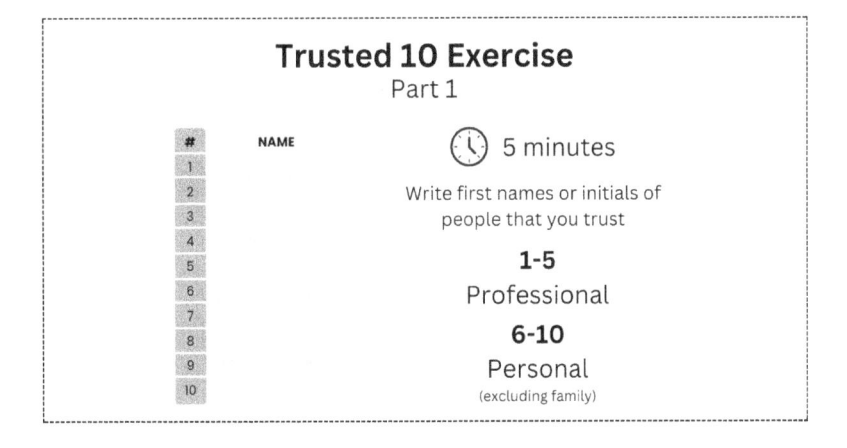

NAME   🕒 5 minutes

Write first names or initials of
people that you trust

1-5
Professional
6-10
Personal
(excluding family)

Figure 3.3. Trusted 10 Exercise Part 1.

Trusted 10 Exercise

There is an exercise which I have been doing in my training for years and which I have delivered to thousands of engineers. It's called the Trusted 10. Firstly, I hand out a sheet of A4 paper containing a grid. The paper is folded over such that only the first column (Name/Initials) is visible for participants.

Part 1 involves asking people to write down the names of people that they trust. I don't define trust for them; this is up to them to identify.

- 1 to 5 list personal contacts you trust (but NOT family)
- 6 to 10 list professional contacts you trust (does not have to be current employer)

We give them a few minutes for this. For Part 2 of the exercise, I ask them to open out their sheets, and they have to codify people based on their diversity, putting in answers against columns for numerous demographics: gender, race/ethnicity, age, sexual orientation, education, disability status, marital status, religion, other.

Trusted 10 Exercise
Part 2

#	NAME	GENDER	RACE	AGE	SEXUAL ORIENTATION	EDUCATION	DISABILITY	MARRIED	RELIGION
1									
2									
3									
4									
5									
6									
7									
8									
9									
10									

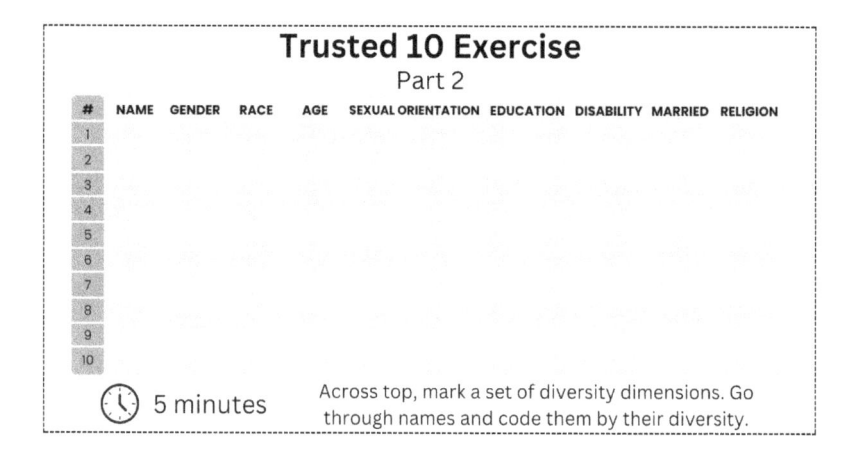

5 minutes — Across top, mark a set of diversity dimensions. Go through names and code them by their diversity.

Figure 3.4. Trusted 10 Exercise Part 2.

Visit the link via the QR code at the end of this chapter for a copy of this exercise for you to try with your teams.

There are numerous learning outcomes from this exercise. I find the following as key observations:

- Participants often find it hard to identify a definition of trust. Some have a different definition for personal contacts than for professional contacts.
- There is a lack of diversity across names listed, with people usually having the same characteristics. Sameness is rife. We do not naturally surround ourselves with people who are **different** to us. Key point is that we have to proactively seek diversity in order to enrich our inner frame of reference. These people will have likely confided in us their secrets, and so we have subconsciously absorbed their biases on the world from their experiences.
- The names some people write down may not stay the same forever. Life events happen. I have had people who are going through a bitter separation where the metaphorical rug has been removed from beneath their feet and who they trust at their point in their life is being tested fundamentally.
- There usually exists a clustering of ages +/- ten years, and this is usually because we are more susceptible to building trusting relationships when we are in our formative years or in a state of needing to build emotional connections personally (e.g., when we start at university, when we relocate with our work, or when we become parents). Once the pattern of our lives set into a rhythm, the less opportunity there is for difference and diversity to enter it.
- You may have marked off what you believe to be the correct answer in relation to someone. But

it might be wrong. For example, you may have identified someone stating that they have no disabilities. But the truth might be that they do and have not shared them with you. The person may be masking, covering, or hiding an aspect of their identity which they have not been truthful about, or may not have even personally explored or discovered about themselves yet.

- There are some diversity dimensions that are still taboo in the workplace setting and so they do not get readily spoken about. Some examples of these "hidden diversity dimensions" include if we follow a religion, or if we have an undisclosed disability status, or even our sexual orientation or gender identity. So, you may not have been able to write an answer because you just do not know.

Trusted 10 Exercise
Part 3

Relationships →
← Diversity

Level 3
- Inner circle / Trusted 10
- Least amount of diversity (for most)

Level 2
- People who are becoming increasingly more trusted
- Moved beyond "I know their name"
- Professional/Personal blend
- Typically, 10% of Level 1

Level 1
- People you are just getting to know
- Acquaintances
- Largest number
- Most diverse group

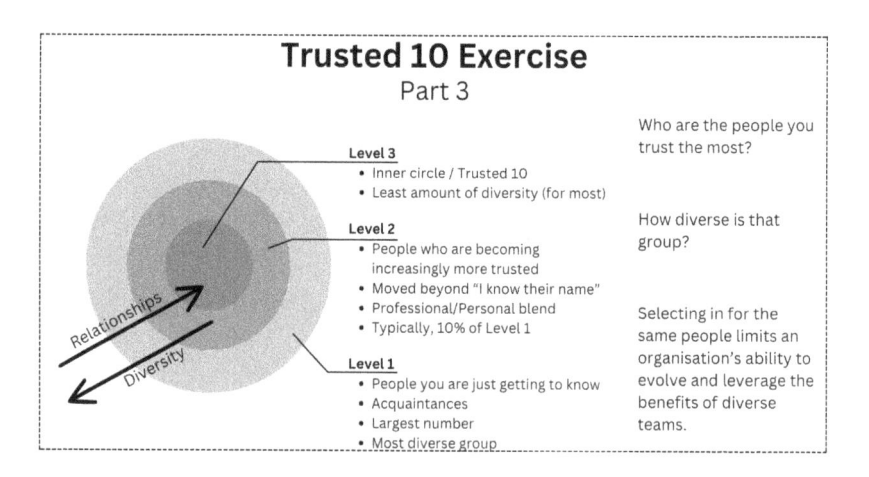

Who are the people you trust the most?

How diverse is that group?

Selecting in for the same people limits an organisation's ability to evolve and leverage the benefits of diverse teams.

Figure 3.5. Trusted 10 Exercise Part 3.

Relationship Level Diagram

We typically have three levels of relationships in life. We have:

- Level 1 – people who you are just getting to know, your acquaintances. This level is the largest and the most diverse group.
- Level 2 – moving beyond "I know their name," becoming increasingly more trusted, and it's a professional/personal blend. Typically 10 percent of level 1.
- Level 3 – your inner circle, your Trusted 10, and for most people, this contains the least amount of diversity.

So our relationships are inversely proportional to diversity.

[Diagram: a curve on axes with the text "So our relationships are inversely proportional to diversity" following the shape of the curve]

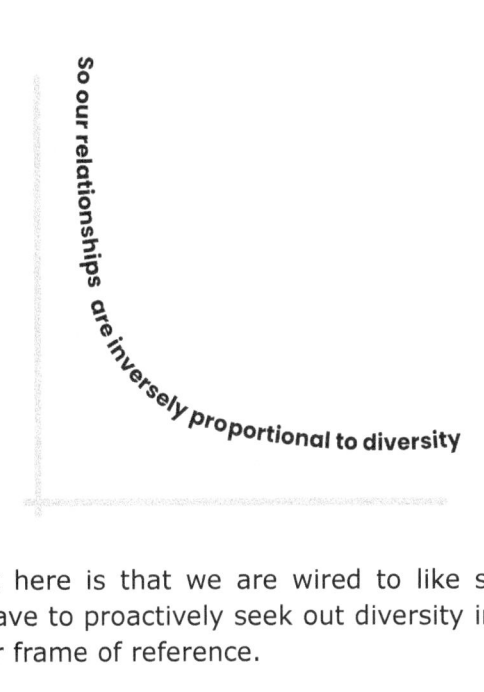

The point here is that we are wired to like sameness, and we have to proactively seek out diversity in order to enrich our frame of reference.

When I set up my LGBTQ+ organisation InterEngineering, I never knowingly knew any transgender people, yet I was setting up a professional network to represent this group. I went and found out firsthand from transgender role models about their experiences and what they have gone through, so much so that I can now be an advocate (confidently) for their needs.

This is the opportunity employee networks allow.

In a business context, if you have an opportunity that lands on your desk, and it has to be delivered on time, on budget, safely, and by yesterday, and it has your professional reputation at stake . . . are you going to give it to someone in your Level 1? Unlikely. More likely your Level 3, or close Level 2.

This opportunity could be the exact thing that someone needs to get that year-end promotion, to prove themselves capable. But because you do not know them, they do not get the opportunity to receive the task.

The privilege could be as simple as people who are always present in the office and not working at home or flexi-time. You do not consciously realise it; we just need to get better at connecting on an interpersonal level.

Case Study

One of my clients was a large travel organisation and they arranged networking drinks between the senior directors and the new graduates who had recently joined. One of the directors had quite a generous budget to commission some new videos to promote the company by using an external media production agency.

At the networking event, one of the new graduates shared that her side hustle was video production and that she was passionate about it. The director offered the graduate to take the project on instead as part of their graduate rotation programme. The graduate went on to deliver such a high-quality product that the company won an award from LinkedIn for Best Growth in customer engagement because the videos were of such good quality, they used it on their platform.

The company delivered the videos at a fraction of the price an external agency would have cost, and they inevitably secured the retention of the graduate in question because they created an alignment between a passion, a skill, and a business need.

The learning output here is that the graduate was in the director's Level 1 relationship circle. And it is unlikely that they would have readily crossed paths through regular business-as-usual activities. It took for the business to proactively create moments for interpersonal connection to occur, and as such there was an opportunity for the graduate to share something with the director about their skills and experience. And with a trusting director who took a low-risk chance, it paid off in dividends.

How often are you putting yourself in situations where you can get to know people who are different from yourself, and get to know them at a level beneath their waterline?

Business leaders need to proactively create disruptive knowledge sharing forums. Investment in team building and social activities are often some of the first things to go when budgets are cut. Yet, in the context of coming out of a global pandemic, the moments for interpersonal connection have been nonexistent. Conversations in coffee rooms, water cooler moments, on lunch breaks, on walks with colleagues, the five minutes before and after meetings. These are the moments where interpersonal connection happens.

In the shift to hybrid working, it is important to make sure we actively cultivate moments for interpersonal connection. And in doing so, create a learning opportunity to get to know people from different backgrounds, cultures, and identities.

Humanising an identity and having role models to anchor your experience is one way to combat biases you will harbour from stereotypes perpetuated in the media, and from stories shared with you across your life.

Diversity Reboots Outdated Operating Systems

If we take the engineering sector's response to Covid-19 as an example of how industries can change their operating systems when they need to, let's consider what current operating system we're using in terms of workplace or learning culture and how we can reset it for the betterment of society.

The pace of change for diversification of the engineering and tech sectors has been glacial. The percentage of women in the engineering workforce has increased from

11 percent in 2011 to 16 percent in 2021.[28] Considering this period is an entire decade, it's a small rate of change.

The engineering sector cannot report data on hidden identities such as sexual orientation, gender identity, disability, and mental health status, simply because we do not ask these questions to determine a baseline. Our datasets on race and ethnicity are also questionable.

This is remarkable considering we are an industry that prides itself on data. We hypothesise what incremental improvements can be made in engineering to improve efficiencies, make gains, and grow productivity. We make those changes and see the impact on our baseline. So, how can we validate whether our interventions have been successful if we do not know our full starting point?

One in six people who are Generation Z adults identify as LGBTQ+.[29] Generation Z will make up over 30 percent of the workforce by 2030 and this number is only going to get larger as we progress through this century. Generation Alpha are those born between the early 2010s to mid 2020s, and Generation Beta are to follow.

As an industry, we need to ask ourselves if the trajectory for the rate of change of our cultural value set is at pace with wider societal changes. Can we be confident we are setting ourselves up for success to attract more talented people into our sector?

---

[28] EngineeringUK, "Trends in the Engineering Workforce."
[29] Nico Lang, "Gen Z is the Queerest Generation According to New Survey," *Them*, February 24, 2021, https://www.them.us/story/gen-z-millennials-queerest-generation-gallup-poll.

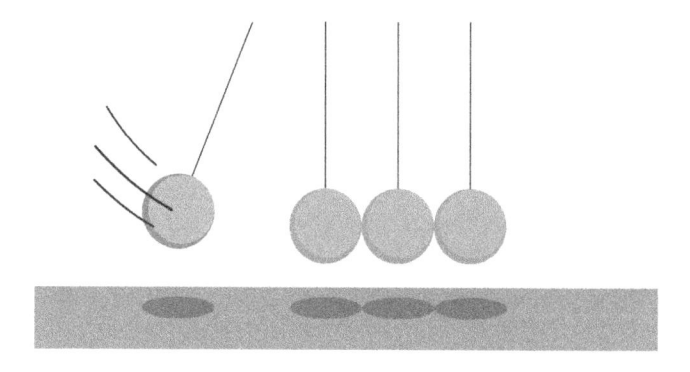

Figure 3.6. Pendulum graphic.

The march towards equity is like a pendulum. If "too much progress" is achieved for minoritised groups in a short space of time, majority groups perceive that too much opportunity has been given out. The metaphorical brakes come on, and we see a swing back in terms of attitudes and possibly even an undoing on rights that have been achieved. The key for social justice movements is not to swing back further than the original, historical starting point.

For example, the London 2012 Olympic Games was designed to be a Games to inspire a whole new generation into sport. I was studying for my PhD at the time, and London was an incredible place to be. The vibe was positive, everyone was incredibly friendly, and diversity was front-and-centre with unity a core value. In the years since, there has been a widening of attitudes. Brexit brought great polarity to the UK, and social justice movements of MeToo and BlackLivesMatter have had an impact. There exists an ongoing tension between the rights of trans* people and some cisgendered women who perceive rights for the trans* community are in conflict with their rights.

With Generation Z identifying as such, and the other generations upcoming, we cannot afford to have cultures in our organisations where people do not feel they will belong. Cultures where they do not see themselves as being represented or where they feel they will have no career progression do not foster a sense of security.

The most pressing issue for humanity right now is addressing the climate crisis. Engineers will be pivotal in creating the solutions that address our biggest challenges, such as climate change, food security, and global health provisions. The timer is ticking, and we need more people training to become specialists in STEM. We cannot afford to exclude qualified individuals or people who have the potential to be excellent STEM professionals. We need all the talent we can get, and right now, we are not getting nearly enough new people on board.

We have huge swathes of industries with collective centuries of experience between employees who are going to retire. We need to create intergenerational connections and not allow biases of one group over another to trip us up from achieving a truly inclusive culture.

The majority group of the current workforce see diversity as an add-on – or something done on the side of the day job – and not as implicit within the role of core engineering and STEM in general. We need to change this assumption to change the Operating System.

Inclusive Engineering Design

One way to change the Operating System is to embed a mindset shift from day one of a future engineer's journey. The world is becoming more globalised every day, meaning solution technologies need building with *everyone* in mind. However, in an industry that's notoriously lacking in diversity, engineers are not designing and building future-proof and inclusive solutions.

The focus is often on what outcome the beneficiary or clients have asked for or need, meaning the development and creativity of a product or solution lacks consideration for those who were not involved in its design.

Due to said lack of diversity in the engineering industry, this often means women, an ageing population, people with disabilities, and those with other underrepresented characteristics do not have a seat at the table when it comes to designing future technologies. This leads to incomplete, exclusive, inaccessible, and unsustainable solutions.

If we are building for a globalised world, we need to make sure we are not only building for a subset of the global population.

> If we are building for a globalised world, we **need** to make sure we are **not only** building for a subset of the global population

Inclusive Engineering Framework

Figure 3.7. Inclusive Engineering Framework[30]

This is where inclusive engineering design comes into play. It aims to include all perspectives and therefore eradicate bias and discrimination (however unconscious) at the design stage. The framework, first proposed by engineer Dawn Bonfield, MBE, FREng, looks at:

1. Putting People at the Heart of Solutions
2. Ethics
3. Global Responsibility and Appropriate Technology
4. Future Technology
5. Societal Impact
6. Sustainable Development Goals
7. Safety and Cyber Security
8. The Natural Environment

---

[30] Dawn Bonfield, "Inclusive Engineering Framework," Towards Vision, https://www.inceng.org/inclusive-engineering-framework.html.

Each of these aspects interlink and foster an ethically minded value shift that puts human-centred design at the forefront. It covers every area of engineering, from artificial intelligence to smart construction, to build solutions that are good for the whole of society, the environment, and the future.

This vision requires the conversation around DEI to start in schools, in universities, and throughout an engineer's career. Including inclusive engineering design in the syllabus is one of the easiest ways to set future engineers up for success.

Globalisation is already happening, and people are already looking for inclusive and innovative solutions to some of the world's biggest threats, such as climate change and pandemics. This cannot happen unless everyone is given a voice. In that vein, inclusive design is a safety issue that goes hand in hand with DEI.

This leads me back to the link between H&S and DEI. Creating a physical and psychologically safe workplace where innovation and inclusive design can flourish is the best way to future-proof your business in a globalised world. Organisations need to factor in psychosocial hazards and risks when doing engineering design. This involves giving due consideration to the process of doing the design, the culture created within the teams designing products and services, who is represented within the team, and whether communities impacted by the design are consulted with. Does there exist a culture where people can openly challenge, if needed, and raise concerns?

A positive physical safety culture encourages people to speak up when they see unsafe acts, things that may put people's lives in danger. A psychologically safe workplace is where people feel empowered to speak out and do not shy away for the fear of ramifications. This is a culture where leadership proactively encourages people to speak out on anything that makes them feel unsafe, and this could be in relation to their identity. Some people may be on the receiving end of microaggressions, seemingly innocuous comments said in jest, but underlying these comments and actions, they are taking a toll on the person or group.

An inclusive design team is one where everyone can share wholeheartedly their inputs, is listened to, feels heard, and is valued for their contributions. The team itself is also representative of broader society and has a diverse mix of experiences, ages, and backgrounds. A team where there is no silencing, no filtering, and no masking.

Can you imagine if there had been greater representation of disabled people within design teams working on built environment projects? Our towns and cities and urban landscapes would look very different because people could have offered their lived experience to influence the design.

Key Takeaways

- Engineering is currently operating in an outdated Operating System and needs an upgrade.

- The Covid-19 pandemic proved how innovation and keeping up with the shifting needs of a workforce leads to better productivity outcomes.

- Women's representation in engineering rose from 11 percent to 16 percent over a decade, marking slow but positive DEI progress.

- By 2030, Generation Z will make up over 30 percent of the workforce, preferring inclusive and diverse work environments.

- For engineering to excel in talent acquisition, diversity must be integral from education to project execution, not a peripheral.

- Inclusive design ensures engineering solutions are suitable for a global and diverse population, future-proofing projects.

Scan now and download the resources from this chapter.

Or visit:
equalengineers.com/TheSAFELeader/downloads

CHAPTER FOUR

Expanding the Operating System to Include Psychological Safety

Improving Mental Health and Well-Being and Reducing the Risk of Suicide Through DEI

Public Health England commissioned research with the Office for National Statistics (ONS) that looked at 18,998 deaths of people aged twenty to sixty-four (a rate of about twelve deaths for every 100,000 people per year) who killed themselves in England between 2011 and 2015.[31] Of these records, 13,232 had information on the deceased's occupation. Suicide is the leading cause of death for men under fifty and about four in five (10,688) deaths included in the analysis were among men.

The ONS found low-skilled male construction workers had the greatest risk, at 3.7 times the national average, and the risk for low-skilled workers in process plant operations was 2.6 times. People in roles such as managers

---

[31] Haroon Siddique, "Male Construction Workers at Greatest Risk of Suicide, Study Finds," *The Guardian*, March 17, 2017, https://www.theguardian.com/society/2017/mar/17/male-construction-workers-greatest-risk-suicide-england-study-finds.

and directors (the highest-paid group) had the lowest risk of suicide.

The workplace offers an opportunity to reach people who need extra support where early intervention is key.

> The workplace offers an *opportunity* to reach people who need extra support where early intervention is **key**

We should treat mental health as seriously as we do physical health and combat it as rigorously too, ending the stigma around disclosure. There are many toolkits available online to achieve this.

A positive example of early workplace intervention is the Time to Change initiative, which ran from 2007 to 2021. It encouraged organisations to adopt its seven key principles:

1. Demonstrate senior-level buy-in;
2. Demonstrate accountability and recruit employee champions;
3. Raise awareness about mental health;
4. Update and implement policies to address mental health problems in the workplace;
5. Ask staff to share personal experiences of mental health problems;
6. Equip line managers to have conversations about mental health; and
7. Provide information about mental health and sign-post to support services.

Although the initiative ran out of funding, it was hugely successful and produced incredibly useful resources, all of which I downloaded and archived in the sad event their website was shut down!

One of its notable achievements was the real change in the discrimination reported by people with lived experience in 2021. Discrimination in employment fell by a quarter (25 percent) and in social life by a third (32 percent) since 2016.

This proves how well-run awareness initiatives create impactful change. Time to Change's social proof is a success story we can use when it comes to creating psychologically safe environments in our workplaces. This brings me onto how we do this. How do we eradicate stigma and create parity between physical and psychological safety?

Mental Health First-Aiders

There are legal requirements around the number of physical first-aiders required for the size of an organisation. This is usually based on a ratio of the number of people in a given office space. These trained first-aiders know how to respond if there's some form of physical injury and are tasked with getting the individual additional medical help (if needed).

Most of us would know how to help if we saw someone having a heart attack – we'd start CPR, or at the very least, call emergency services. But too few of us would know how to respond if we saw someone having a panic attack or if we were concerned that a friend or coworker might be showing signs of alcoholism.

Mental health first aid takes the fear and hesitation out of starting conversations about mental health and substance use problems by improving understanding and providing an action plan that teaches people to safely and responsibly identify and address a potential mental illness or substance use disorder.

When more people are equipped with the tools they need to start a dialogue, more people can get the help they need. Mental health first-aiders are a vital link between someone experiencing a mental health or substance use challenge and appropriate supports. Companies should establish mental health first-aiders in the same ratio as physical first-aiders. However, there is no legal requirement for a mental health first aid training provision. This is a significant oversight that I believe needs to change. The mental health of employees is just as important as physical health. If someone is not mentally their best self at work, they will be ineffective in their job and have low productivity. It is particularly alarming when you consider these could also be the operators of high-risk activities which require focus and attention. We cannot afford for people to not be fully present in their workplace. Expending energy masking, covering, or hiding is not good for the employee and not good for the organisation.

In the UK, 914,000 people suffered work-related stress, depression, or anxiety in 2021/22, which was a contributing factor to the £18.8 billion estimated cost of injuries and ill health from current working conditions.[32] Better early interventions, a more open culture, and effective signposting will go some way to improving these statistics.

Mental Health First Aid (MHFA) England's mission is to train one in ten adults in mental health awareness and

---

[32] "Health & Safety Statistics," Health & Safety Executive.

skills. They work with over 20,000 employers to achieve this and are slowly raising awareness of mental health in the workplace. One of their pieces of training is to formally train people to become certified mental health first-aiders.

An organisation can then highlight these people through communications on their intranet sites and with photographs stationed around the office showing people's names. The individuals can be demarcated with flags at their desks and can personally wear lanyards, usually a lime green colour with "Mental Health First Aider" printed on them. They can also have their names made known on mental health first aid posters alongside regular physical first-aiders.

MHFA America runs courses that teach you how to identify, understand, and respond to signs of mental illnesses and substance use disorders. The training gives you the skills you need to reach out and provide initial help and support to someone who may be developing a mental health or substance use problem or experiencing a crisis. In the United States, 15,000 instructors have trained more than 2.5 million people.[33] Companies can implement or deepen this network however they see fit. It should work as a complementary service to a formal Employee Assistance Programme (EAP), which is a service usually provided by organisations for employees to confidentially call and report any issues that include their physical or mental health.

It's important to recognise that the role of mental health first-aiders is for them to be on standby, ready to respond in the event someone feels they need support.

---

[33] "About MHFA," Mental Health First Aid, https://www.mentalhealth firstaid.org/about/.

It's generally a role people will take on willingly and voluntarily on top of their day job. **They are not to be considered replacements for a suitably qualified counsellor, capable HR team, or occupational Health & Safety team.** Any ongoing support offered by mental health first-aiders will be at their own discretion, and it's critical they create boundaries when taking on the role, remaining tuned in to when their own ability to support is becoming compromised.

Destigmatising the Discussion around Mental Ill-Health

Mental heath first-aiders' presence and utilisation alone will help destigmatise conversations around mental ill-health in the workplace. They often help start conversations around topics bubbling under the surface that aren't being verbalised but affect the tranches of the workforce. Subjects such as **menopause, men's mental health, fertility journeys, being a carer, and so many other topics are increasingly getting airtime**, leading to people feeling empowered to be open about hidden aspects of their lives or identity.

> ### Case Study: Dave's Story
>
> During a leadership meeting, Dave asked to be excused as he needed to leave the meeting early. Although it was abrupt, no one said anything and the meeting carried on.
>
> Dave took the following days off and when he returned to work, it transpired he was going through a miscarriage with his wife but hadn't spoken about it. Two others in the team confessed to having experienced

> fertility issues and early pregnancy loss within the last few years but had never spoken about it.
>
> At first, the team was shocked that none of them had been able to be open about this with one another, leading to a further concern that with such a high number of cases within their small group, how many more cases are going unreported across the workforce?
>
> This led to the creation of a Parents & Carers Network within the organisation, which evolved to encompass journeys into parenthood as well. The network went on to recognise the need to offer bereavement leave for employees going through the experience, which the company then put in place.

Outcomes like this help raise the visibility that you take the mental health of your employees seriously. Furthermore, it increases the likelihood of earlier intervention since people are more likely to open up when they know they're in a supportive environment.

Mental Health and Psychological Safety

Psychological safety is a term that was first coined by Amy C. Edmundson – professor of leadership and management at Harvard University – in her 1999 article: "**Psychological Safety and Learning Behavior in Work Teams**."[34]

---

[34] Amy Edmondson, "Psychological Safety and Learning Behavior in Work Teams," Administrative Science Quarterly 44, no. 2, (June 1999): https://doi.org/10.2307/2666999.

She defines it as:

> "Psychological safety means an absence of interpersonal fear. When psychological safety is present, people are able to speak up with work-relevant content."

Since the emergence of this term as a team construct, it's gone on to feature as an aspirational workplace culture, which strives to create an environment where people are fully present in the workplace. It underpins a culture of productivity, where outputs are optimised because every contributor is performing at their peak.

Psychological safety requires an establishment of trust between team members across an organisation and up and down a hierarchy.

> **Psychological safety requires an establishment of trust between team members across an organisation and UP and DOWN a hierarchy**

* * * * *

Case Study

It's a cold winter's day and I am delivering our training session on inclusive cultures at a railway depot just outside London to a group comprised of four male engineers. Arms crossed, bodies closed, the group clearly does **not** want to be here. One of them had to be metaphorically dragged in by the HR representative and told to stay. I say to them sarcastically, "*Goooooood morning!* I am not holding you hostage. You can leave if you wish."

The team stays and the session begins. As the session unfolds, their body language changes, their physicality opening up more. And one of the engineers, Jason, shares that his wife who is Polish is feeling anxious. It is around the time of the vote on the UK leaving the European Union, and the ambiguity around Brexit. And she does not know what that means. Is she going to be deported? Is she going to get indefinite leave to remain? Is she going to have the right to work? Are they going to have to spend a lot of time apart?

The ambiguity swirls in her mind and she cannot contain it.

Jason contains it for her.

He is an outlet for her when at home. And then when he comes into the workplace, he stays silent. Like a vessel, pressure rising, but Jason does not talk about it. He does not share it with his colleagues.

One of his colleagues, Brandon, in the training room also at the session for the past few months has just been going on and on and on about Brexit, about how it is not that much of an issue. And in that moment, in the training, Jason turns to Brandon and says "I have had ENOUGH of you. You are really PISSING me off. You have no idea what I am going through at home right now. My wife is in tears, and then I come here, into work, and you are just push-push-push. I have had enough."

> The room goes quiet. I draw Jason's attention back to me and I acknowledge him. I say thank you, thank you for sharing that, that was brave. Finally, he felt heard by the group with what he shared.
>
> The guys came up to me at the end of the session and thanked me, saying they were not expecting to get what they got out of the session.
>
> This is an extract from my keynote talk which I delivered in New York, a copy of this can be accessed by scanning the QR code at the end of this chapter.

I knew I was on to something here, and so I acted. I rewrote all our training content. I decided to centre the discussion not on minoritised groups but on getting the voice of the white, cisgendered, heterosexual, nondisabled, neurotypical male engineers who represent the majority of the engineering profession.

The usual approach to date of centring on minoritised groups makes the majority group feel threatened. The conversation then quickly disintegrates into "When is International Men's Day?" etc. We are having conversations on strategies that are having shallow impact. We are not having transformative change and are instead stuck with no way forward. Men are being silent as they do not see what their role is in this new, inclusive world. They simply feel they are being told that they are the problem.

This is why language is important and why we have to assume positive intent and "call people in" as opposed to "calling people out." Calling out is useful when you need to let someone know their behaviour is unacceptable, or when it must be interrupted to avoid causing more harm. This is also a signal to the wider community.

Calling in is useful if you want to engage someone in a deeper discussion, understanding, and reflection.[35] It involves listening as well as feedback in a two-way conversation.

My strategy therefore with rewriting our content was not to avoid the conversation on misogyny, homophobia, biphobia, transphobia, racism, ableism (etc.) within engineering, not to diminish those voices, but instead to start from a different point. **By starting the discussion with the alarming rates of mental ill-health and suicidal ideation we had uncovered, which disproportionately affect men, it helps the male majority understand that an inclusive culture is also about them**.

It helps them see that a culture where they can challenge toxic masculinity and learn to share their feelings can benefit them. Men can be vulnerable too. As the layers of the conversation are peeled back like an onion and case studies of groups who are marginalised in STEM are introduced, learners go into listening mode. They absorb the content, reflect on it, and apply it to their workplace context and both personal and professional lives.

This approach deescalates and is a depolarising way to have the conversation about the need for greater DEI in STEM. Men hear about the role they can play and understand that they have power and privilege through representation as a majority group, that their voices can access settings that others (currently) cannot. We are rewriting the playbook of how to engage the majority faster and more efficiently, so we can spend more time on the real work: inspiring cultures where caustic leadership styles are replaced with inclusive leadership traits.

---

[35] "Call Out and Call in Racism," Creative Equity Toolkit, https://creativeequitytoolkit.org/topic/anti-racism/call-out-call-in-racism.

The SAFE Leader© Model

In today's rapidly evolving world, the demand for inclusive and empathetic leadership in STEM is more pressing than ever. To address this need, I present the SAFE Leader Model – a dynamic framework designed to foster a culture of inclusivity, understanding, and empowerment in any organisation.

Our SAFE Leader© model is an important framework for this.

Share	At the heart of inclusive leadership lies the power of sharing. This element emphasises the importance of open communication, where SAFE Leaders share their experiences, insights, and vulnerabilities. It's not just about speaking; it's about creating a space where every voice is heard and valued. Sharing fosters trust, builds empathy, and sets the stage for genuine connections within the team.
Act	Inclusive leadership requires action. This component of the SAFE Leader model underscores the need for proactive measures to build an inclusive environment. It's about taking deliberate steps to advocate for underrepresented groups, implement equitable practices, and challenge the status quo. Action translates good intentions into meaningful change.
Feel	The ability to empathise with others is a cornerstone of effective leadership. "Feel" encourages SAFE Leaders to develop a deep understanding of their team members' perspectives and emotions. It's about creating an emotionally intelligent leadership style that resonates with the needs and feelings of everyone in the organisation.

Empower	The final pillar of the SAFE Leader model is about empowering individuals and teams. Empowerment in this context means equipping people with the tools, confidence, and autonomy to contribute their best. It's about creating an environment where individuals feel supported and valued, enabling them to thrive and grow.

The SAFE Leader Model is more than a set of principles; it's a commitment to nurturing a workspace where diversity is celebrated, voices are heard, and everyone has the opportunity to excel. As we delve deeper into each of these components, we'll explore how they can be effectively implemented to create a truly inclusive and dynamic leadership environment in STEM.

SAFE — Share, Act, Feel, Empower

Figure 4.1. SAFE description graphic.
Visit QR code at the end of this chapter for information on our SAFE Leader training course.

Unconscious Bias

In order to become a SAFE Leader, we first need to go back to some fundamentals on how we have evolved to become who we are, and how our brain guides us to make the decisions we make, both rationally and irrationally.

Professor Steve Peters explores the concept of us having two sides to our brain: our human brain and our chimp brain.[36] Our chimp brain is our core amygdala and the inner voice we hear when faced with new information. It drives our fight-or-flight response and is a residue from our past, where we had to immediately respond when faced with danger: run or be eaten. When we outwardly react to the responses coming from our chimp brain, we can be irrational and biased. This is also known as **unconscious bias**.

There has been a movement in DEI programmes to educate people on unconscious bias. The idea here is that we all have biases impacting our judgment and decision-making. The key is being aware of what biases we have and recognising when they may be playing a part in us making a decision. We can then seek out countermeasures to eradicate their impact.

---

[36] Steve Peters, *The Chimp Paradox* (New York: TarcherPerigee, 2013).

Bias Type	Description
Conformity Bias	Caused by group peer pressure (e.g., one person on an interview panel may go along with the majority opinion, even if they feel differently).
Beauty Bias	We think that the most physically attractive person will be the most successful.
Affinity Bias	We find an instant connection with someone (e.g., university, hometown, hobbies, or they remind us of a friend).
Halo Effect	We see one great thing about a person, which affects our opinions of everything else about them (e.g., they are a top highlight, attend a top university, or got a top grade).
Horns Effect	We see one "bad" thing about a person and it sticks (e.g., we might be put off if they speak with a regional accent which may be associated with intelligence, and this clouds everything else).
Similarity Bias	We like people who are like us.
Contrast Effect	Interviewers compare a candidate with the person who was interviewed directly before them.
Attribution Bias	Systematic errors made when we evaluate or try to find reasons for others' behaviours (e.g., if someone has done something well, we consider them lucky, but if they've done something badly we tend to think it's due to their personality or bad behaviour).

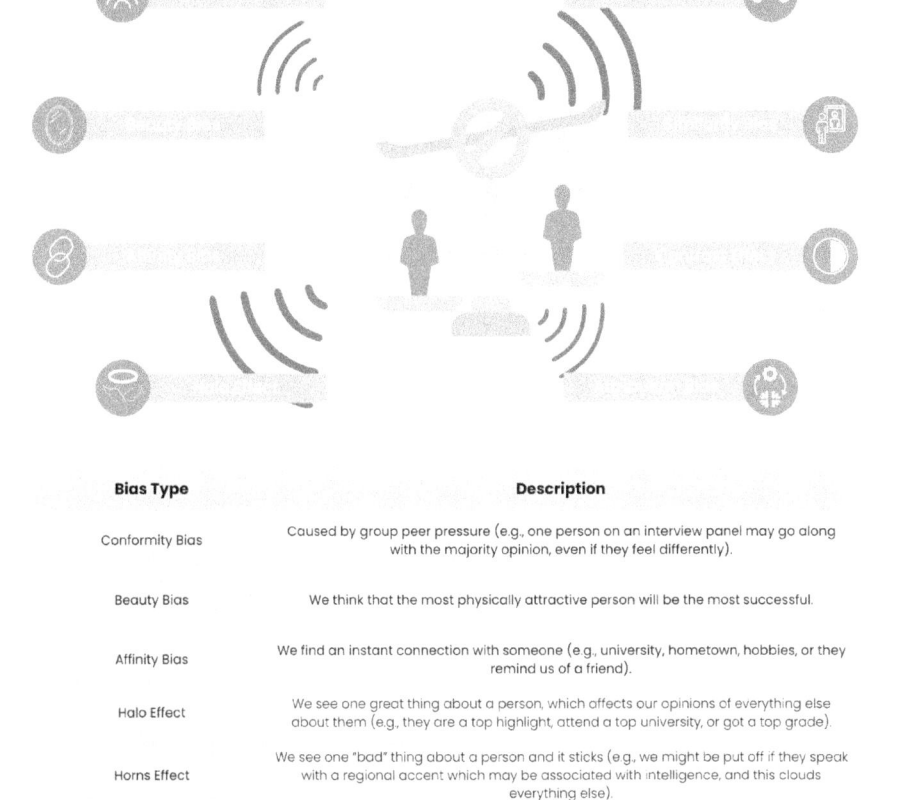

Figure 4.2. Descriptions of Types of Bias[37]

---

[37] Mark McBride-Wright, "Health & Safety: Diverse & Inclusive," The Chemical Engineer Magazine, July 20, 2017, https://www.thechemicalengineer.com/features/health-and-safety-diverse-and-inclusive/.

Hundreds of biases exist, ranging from conformity bias caused by group peer pressure; affinity bias when we meet someone we have a connection with; and confirmation bias where we subconsciously look for evidence to back up our preconceived opinions of someone.

Unconscious bias training aims to make you aware (consciously) of your cognitive biases and suggest mechanisms to reduce people's biases affecting their decision-making. In the workplace, this could be blind recruitment practices and panel interviews (instead of one-on-one).

Although it's a worthy goal, some organisations hold unconscious bias training in the hopes it'll fix their DEI issues. However, it's just one tool within a suite of tools that needs utilising. A one-hour lunch and learn or an early-morning breakfast meeting is a good way to introduce the concept to the workforce, but the conversation needs continuing through regular, ongoing training – especially for people managers and those involved in recruitment.

It's worth noting the feeling amongst some DEI practitioners that unconscious bias training can backfire; people roll their eyes when you mention it, and general fatigue around the concept exists. Hearing how others are biased and that it's "natural" to stereotype, people feel less motivated to change their behaviours and become more inclusive. Consequently, unconscious bias training should bring the existence of biases to people's attention alongside the introduction of mechanisms to reduce its impact – ideally within a robust DEI strategy.

How DEI Tackles Unconscious Bias

We're all shaped by our experiences and environment. Our opinions and values come from the things that are most important to us, and as none of us walk in each other's shoes, what we care about varies. Of course, when it comes to certain groups, for example, LGBTQIA+ (Lesbian, Gay, Bisexual, Transgender, Queer and/or Questioning, Intersex, Asexual and/or Allies), ethnic minority, neurodivergent or disabled people, there is a shared experience. But ultimately, even within these groups, every individual's perspective is unique. How our identities and experiences intersect is complex and entirely personal.

The unconscious bias training that currently exists can be useful in tackling the issues associated with stereotypes; however, the sense of fatigue on this subject – especially in the engineering industry – means unconscious bias training suffers from poor engagement. No one likes to admit fault, and people are tired of being told they're biased. Also, when we tell people how "everyone does it," we unwittingly normalise harmful behaviours.

We need to reimagine how we present unconscious bias training and use a supporting DEI strategy instead.

> We need to reimagine how we present **unconscious bias training and use a supporting DEI strategy instead**

Diversity itself reveals the differences between people; a mix of backgrounds in an organisation does more to evidence diversity than a tick in an ethics box. So, we need to introduce unconscious bias training as a *supplement* to a robust and holistic DEI strategy. That way, we present the concept to our workforce and begin to evidence its prevalence.

When it's fresh in people's minds and there's an organisational conversation around its impact, mechanisms for reducing the effects of unconscious bias can then be introduced – for example, through bystander training (see chapter 7), refresher training, lunch and learn sessions, inclusive spaces, and morning meetings within key departments like HR and recruitment. At EqualEngineers, we have also had success in our flagship Pathways Programme, where we run a reciprocal mentoring programme where a professional engineer from industry is paired up with an engineering student.

Our programme partners include large organisations such as Network Rail, Rolls-Royce, Airbus, and the UK Atomic Energy Authority (UKAEA). At time of writing, we have taken over 300 students through mentoring opportunities in the space of two years, across three cohorts. We were oversubscribed when we launched in 2021 with over 800 applications. Diversity statistics have been impressive with: 78 percent ethnic minority; 40 percent women; 10 percent lesbian, gay, bisexual; 8 percent disabled; 5 percent neurodivergent; 2 percent transgender; and 1 percent nonbinary.

Intergenerational boundaries are shattered, biases are challenged, and community is built. This is making it real. It engages the male-majority workforce because they have a chance to meet an upcoming engineer, and they feel valuable imparting information and insights from their career. There is also a level of trust that is built where people feel comfortable sharing their concerns, or what they do not know about certain topics. It humanises relationships, fosters connection, challenges cultural stereotypes, and helps close the skills gap in STEM. Visit the link via the QR code at the end of this chapter for more information.

The aim is to create an organisation that recognises disparity and supports parity for greater and fairer

- job prospects,
- promotional opportunities,
- innovation,
- workplace culture,
- team performance,
- Health & Safety, and
- education

for everyone who works there.

> **Unconscious Bias Case Study: Fred's Story**
>
> Fred wanted to improve his understanding of DEI, so he attended a training course run by EqualEngineers called "Engaging the Majority." The aim of the course was to offer valuable insight into how to improve attendees' diversity and inclusion efforts. Fred explored themes such as resilience, unconscious bias, privilege, and microaggressions to better understand his own contributions to the lack of diversity in his organisation.
>
> Fred is a shy person who didn't have much exposure to diverse groups growing up. He felt happy to go to work on the construction site, do his job, and go home

at the end of the day. However, he worked in a team of five with one colleague called Darren, who was openly gay. Fred didn't know Darren was gay until the other members of the team started making crude jokes about it. Fred found it uncomfortable but didn't say anything. Then, one day, Darren didn't show up for work. The other members of the team didn't worry; however, Fred wondered if their bullying was the reason for Darren's absence. He raised his concerns with his supervisor, who called Darren and discussed the problem at hand. It turned out Fred was right, further discovering how Darren feared for his safety on site because of the lack of respect or unity from his teammates. He felt scared to ask for help or raise concerns.

During the training with EqualEngineers, Fred spoke about his shyness and revealed how he had an undiagnosed neurodiversity. When the trainer reflected this back at him regarding Darren, he realised how Darren also struggled to fit in, feel valued, and feel safe in his workplace. In other words, his own diversity story helped him empathise with Darren's.

Understanding how Darren felt unsafe due to the unconscious (and some very conscious!) bias surrounding him helped Fred put things into perspective. When he returned to the site, he revealed his neurodiversity to Darren and they agreed to look out for each other. Not only that, but the rest of the team stopped making crude jokes and noticed a difference in how Darren approached his job.

All names in this case study have been changed to protect individual identities.

The Importance of Equality for Psychological Safety

In the UK, engineering has an 84 percent male majority workforce, which demonstrates the lack of women in the profession. A 2010 study illustrated that teams containing more women demonstrated greater social sensitivity and, in turn, greater collective intelligence compared to teams containing fewer women.[38]

Diversity programmes in engineering and technology have typically focussed on getting more women into the industries because, statistically, they're the largest group from wider society who are underrepresented across the workforce. However, majority groups often feel excluded in the push for greater diversity.

Having more women in a team encourages collective sensitivity and increases a team's emotional intelligence. Men don't tend to speak about their problems; they bottle them up and let them fester, and a majority-male workforce results in fewer men opening up about anything negative going on in their lives.

To reiterate: Engineering places a strong emphasis on physical safety but far less on psychological safety.

Recall that suicide is the highest killer of men under 45, and in the construction, process, and manufacturing industries, a male worker is more likely to die through

---

[38] "Collective Intelligence: Number of Women in Group Linked to Effectiveness in Solving Difficult Problems," *Science Daily*, October 2, 2010, https://www.sciencedaily.com/releases/2010/09/100930143 339.htm.

suicide than a typical process safety hazard like a dropped object falling from a height or electrocution.[39]

This means engineering organisations are failing to minimise the highest cause of death of their workforce: suicide. Although they've done well to improve LTIRs because of physical safety, what are they doing to ensure psychological safety too? The brain is also an organ and deserves the same respect as the rest of our body. Mental health first aid training needs to form part of the solution.

The Importance of DEI for Psychological Safety

I believe we're currently missing a huge opportunity to ameliorate our industry.

The intention of diversity, equity, inclusion, and belonging programmes are often positioned through phrases such as "bringing your whole self to work" or "be your full, authentic self in the workplace and thrive." However, despite the intention of our inclusion and belonging programmes to achieve this, there is a big disconnect with the way our male-majority workforce is experiencing these efforts. For example, if the male majority were bringing their full selves to work, they'd exist in a workplace that allowed them to be open about any root causes of mental ill-health and/or suicidal ideation.

---

[39] "Suicide by Occupation, England & Wales, 2011 to 2020 Registrations," Office for National Statistics, https://www.ons.gov.uk/peoplepopulationandcommunity/birthsdeathsandmarriages/deaths/adhocs/13674suicidebyoccupationenglandandwales2011to2020registrations.

Consequently, **diversity, equity, inclusion, and belonging are about psychological safety**. I believe we can use this hook to create the quintuple win of:

1. Dramatically reducing loss of life due to suicide
2. Making engineering more inclusive
3. Increasing the attractiveness of the industry to work within
4. Retaining the existing talent we've worked hard to develop, and
5. Increasing productivity and performance at scale by shifting engineering from a culturally laggard position to one known for innovation, being cutting edge, and having a positive impact on society

Recommendations: How to Improve Mental Health in the Engineering Sector

Now we've discussed the links between DEI, Inclusive H&S, and mental health, creating a robust strategy comprised of all these elements requires a shift in focus. Within a male-majority industry and organisation, connecting and implementing a strategy that focuses on "inclusion" that benefits **everyone** will help tackle the issue. We will do this by:

1. Creating parity of esteem between physical safety and mental health to address the mental ill-health emergency
2. Enabling a "personable" culture in engineering so people are more comfortable talking about what is going on in their lives
3. Increasing the dialogue on stress, depression, and mental, physical, and financial health issues (which have been exacerbated by Covid-19) and putting support mechanisms in place

4. Employing strong and consistent messaging about DEI programmes to get buy-in from all employees and achieve the intended objectives
5. Keeping a tab on employees' physical and mental health by looking for any red flags by having an employer/employee support programme in place

The next two chapters are going to explore some core fundamental concepts in safety management involving the Bradley Curve. We will consider how it applies to physical safety and then how we can adapt it as a model for building psychological safety into our workplace cultures. We will go deeper into the SAFE Leader© model and how it can be used to engineer inclusive cultures.

Key Takeaways

- Psychological safety removes fear from interpersonal interactions, fostering open communication.

- Our primal instincts contribute to unconscious biases, affecting judgment and decisions.

- Recognising biases in our decision-making helps counter their normalisation and promotes collective change, rather than accepting "everyone does it" as an excuse.

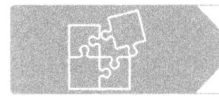

- Unconscious bias training alone cannot eradicate bias, especially because of the fatigue people feel on the subject. It's one piece of a holistic DEI strategy.

- Mentoring is a powerful tool in breaking down boundaries between generations and challenging cultural stereotypes.

- DEI tackles unconscious bias by helping eradicate the groupthink mentality of majority teams that lack diversity.

- DEI enhances psychological safety by including women, fostering open discussions and addressing higher suicide rates among men.

- Studies show how equality in teams encourages more empathetically led discussions.

Scan now and download the resources from this chapter.

Or visit:
equalengineers.com/TheSAFELeader/downloads

CHAPTER FIVE

A New Inclusive Operating System: The Bradley Curve Revisited

Important: For those unfamiliar with the Bradley Curve, this section is an essential read. Not only is the Bradley Curve an incredibly useful tool for telling the story of how safety culture has improved, but I revisit the concept throughout the book, building upon it to help embed a DEI strategy in your organisation that *actually* works.

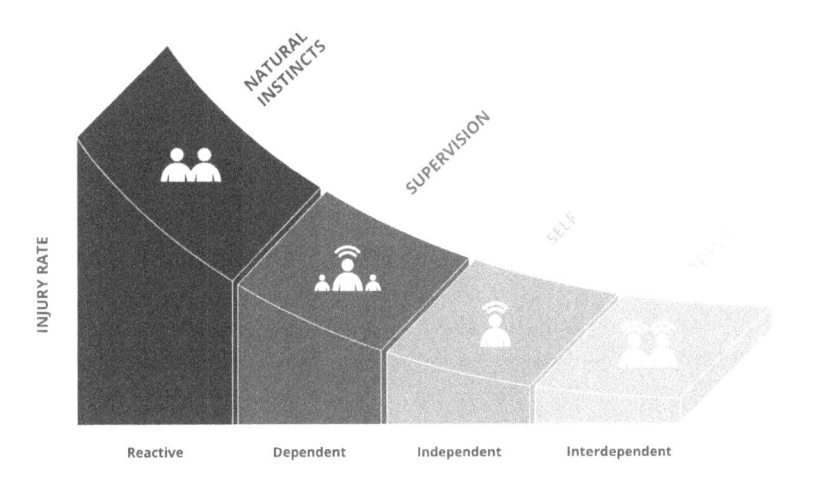

Figure 5.1. 4-Step Bradley Curve.

Figure 5.1 shows the stages of physical safety and the associated motivations within the workplace cultures.

Dr. H. James Bradley, a process safety engineer, first developed the Bradley Curve in the early 1980s as a way to understand the root causes of accidents and incidents in the chemical and process industries. Also known as the Incident Investigation Curve or Safety Performance Curve, the concept was intended to help businesses identify the relationship between the frequency and severity of accidents or incidents in a system or organisation.

It was widely believed most accidents were caused by human error. Due to the lack of focus on identifying and addressing the underlying organisational contributors to these accidents, Dr. Bradley came up with the Bradley Curve to help businesses do just that. It's a tool that bases its assumptions on a chain of events instead of a single cause. In doing so, organisations can pinpoint and analyse all the risk factors at every stage of their manifestation, which in turn helps them build strategies for mitigating these risks. It's particularly useful when it comes to understanding and managing risks in complex systems and organisations.

The Bradley Curve is established by plotting the frequency of accidents on the x-axis and the severity on the y-axis. Four quadrants represent each stage of an accident, from the latent conditions that led to an accident to the consequences of that accident. The four quadrants are: Natural Instinct, Supervision, Self, and Teams. An organisation's goal is to build a clear picture of how accidents occur and look at ways to minimise the risks.

Let's take a closer look at the four quadrants below.

1) Culture: Reactive – Motivation: Natural Instinct

Humans respond to hazards and risks in a workplace context because of our gut and natural reactions as human beings when there is a risk of physical injury.

> **Example:** You're on a construction site in Manchester in the North West of England, visiting one of your clients on a large construction project for which you are a project engineer.
>
> You're walking under some scaffolding with some workers working at height some distance above your head. You have all your Personal Protective Equipment (PPE) on, including steel toe cap boots, Hi-Vis overalls, protective glasses, and a hard hat.
>
> You're mid-conversation with a colleague when you suddenly hear the clattering of metal hitting metal, immediately followed by loud shouts from above. You instinctively run under the scaffolding, out of the open area at the bottom, and pull your colleague in with you.
>
> Moments later, a large spanner lands next to where you were both originally standing. This is an example of a dropped object resulting in a near-miss incident. Your natural reactions are what resulted in you preserving your physical safety.

2) Culture: Dependent – Motivation: Supervision

Humans prioritise safety because we're told it's an imperative. Expectations are set and rules and procedures underwrite an expected code of conduct. Noncompliance can result in disciplinary measures.

Example: You are a civil engineer working on a project improving water drainage as part of a redevelopment project in your local city, Newcastle in the North East of England. You arrive at work and reverse park your car because that is the company's policy to minimise the risk of running someone over when reversing out of a space. You have a 9:00 a.m. meeting with your client.

Your client is the local authority, and the project engineer is visiting your offices for a progress update meeting. You meet them at reception where they have to check in, do their security orientation, and receive their visitors' badge. However it is company policy that they are still required to be escorted throughout their visit due to security sensitivities.

The client has watched the safety induction video upon arrival and has signed an acknowledgement to abide by the safety requirements set out. One of the largest sources of workplace accidents is slips, trips, and falls.

You take the client for a coffee in the local cafe inside your building and, before leaving, you make sure they have put a lid on their coffee cup. It is company policy when walking up and down a staircase to walk on the right hand side and to hold the handrail. Failure to comply with this rule within the company can lead to formal warnings. As the person hosting the visitors to the office, it is also your duty to ensure they abide by the rules and regulations of your organisation. However, you do feel like a teacher asking someone to hold the handrail, and so you do not always do it.

Walking with their coffee in one hand, your client starts ascending the stairs **not** holding on to the handrail. Your client is wearing leather-soled shoes and as they start to walk up, they slip and miss a footing, trip forwards, and prevent themselves from hitting their head on the upper stairs by putting out their hand.

Luckily the lid was on the coffee cup, otherwise this near-miss could have led to someone getting burned. This is a learning moment to reinforce why the company has the policies it has in place, and a reminder to yourself to always speak up no matter how infantile you may feel.

3) Culture: Independent – Motivation: Self

Humans proactively seek out and create safe workplace cultures because it benefits us, we become committed, and are motivated from within. As we care about our self-preservation, it becomes part of our practice and habits as we go about our work.

Example: You are a graduate chemical engineer who has just started in your new graduate role on an exciting project helping produce hydrogen, part of a new colocated project on the South Coast of the United Kingdom, near Southampton. This is part of the government's push towards reaching net-zero carbon emissions, securing more sustainable fuel sources to help combat climate change. You were one of the few women on your course whilst studying your degree. You are excited to be joining industry but are aware of the fact you are in a minority group as most of the workforce is still male. This does not bother you, and you have been an active supporter for gender equality throughout your university years.

As part of your onboarding, you are given some second-hand PPE; however, the boots are too large and the overalls are dirty, worn, and ill-fitting on some parts of your body.

You read an article highlighting the general heightened risk women face whilst on site due to ill-fitting PPE, purely because what's readily available is centred on the proportions of the male body. This is notwithstanding the fact that the PPE you have been given is unsafe and should be taken out of service.

You're not willing to work in an environment where you're at a heightened risk compared to your male colleagues, so you source specialist PPE from a supplier who caters for women.

4) Culture: Interdependent – Motivation: Teams

Humans care for others, have pride in their organisations, and are empowered to call out unsafe acts without fear of retribution.

We know how to respond if someone's physical safety is at risk.

> **Example:** It is a dark, misty evening and you are based in an engineering office in Swansea on the South Coast of Wales. You're in the office and it's been a long day.
>
> Your colleague has been complaining during the latter part of the afternoon about having a migraine. As you both must deliver a project milestone by the following morning, you've both stayed late to get the work over the line.
>
> Your colleague lives further away than you and says they're feeling fine and the migraine has subsided. However, you recognise the signs that it hasn't; for example, they're still wincing, have an eye twitch, and are holding their forehead.
>
> As a result, you're not comfortable letting your colleague drive home on their own in the dark. Instead, you insist that you take them home, make sure they get in okay, and speak with their partner to let them know what has happened.
>
> The well-being of your colleague plays on your mind, and you continue to keep in touch, and ask to be kept informed should anything escalate.

The above is an example of someone's physical safety being considered. However, **do we always know how to respond to mental health emergencies**, such as when someone is having a panic attack, a breakdown, or using language insinuating suicidal ideation?

Reactive vs. Interdependent Culture

A reactive culture is one where there's no proactivity and we're constantly in fight-or-flight mode when it comes to any emergencies, stress, or tension that arises. We've been conditioned to respond to situations based on our experiences from our past and learned behaviours.

In short: We react unconsciously instead of out of considered reflection.

> In short:
> We react **_unconsciously_** instead of out of considered reflection

On the contrary, interdependent cultures involve us speaking out to others proactively. People do it because it's in the role of being a good person. However, not everyone is motivated like this. Reframing intervening in such a way that makes it explicit it's beneficial *for us personally* will help more people do it. Most people are quicker to act when they see personal benefit, and so making obvious the personal gain for helping others may lead to more people doing it. In other words, tapping into everyone's instinctual chimp brain to make it worth their while is more likely to yield results.

Consequently, I'm proposing we consider a new stage to the Bradley Curve called **Inclusive Interdependence**. This frames the inherent benefits to oneself through being proactive in looking out for others. You are not just doing it because it is a good, righteous thing to do, you are doing it to protect yourself. We are driving up collective good behaviour at the system level.

→ Inclusive Interdependence ↩

The Bradley Curve and Psychological Safety

Proposed Physical vs. Psychological Manifestations of the Bradley Curve in Teams

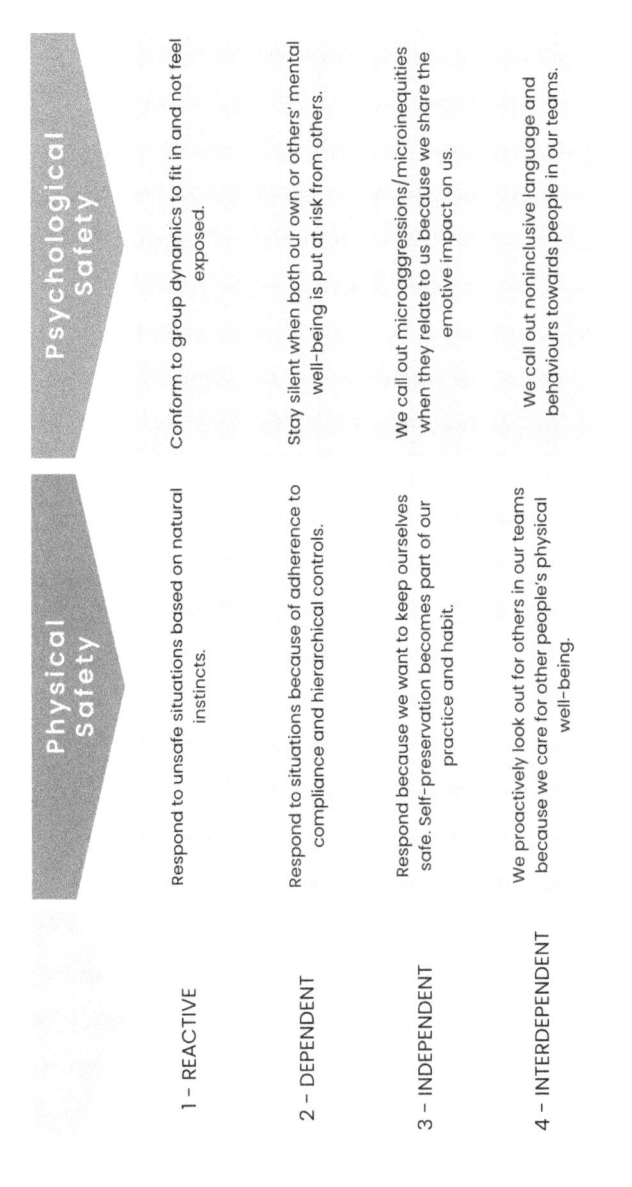

	Physical Safety	Psychological Safety
1 – REACTIVE	Respond to unsafe situations based on natural instincts.	Conform to group dynamics to fit in and not feel exposed.
2 – DEPENDENT	Respond to situations because of adherence to compliance and hierarchical controls.	Stay silent when both our own or others' mental well-being is put at risk from others.
3 – INDEPENDENT	Respond because we want to keep ourselves safe. Self-preservation becomes part of our practice and habit.	We call out microaggressions/microinequities when they relate to us because we share the emotive impact on us.
4 – INTERDEPENDENT	We proactively look out for others in our teams because we care for other people's physical well-being.	We call out noninclusive language and behaviours towards people in our teams.

Figure 5.2. Physical vs. Psychological Manifestations of the Bradley Curve in Teams.

Psychological safety is about ensuring a culture where people feel able to speak up. They're comfortable that when they share their thoughts or feelings, or when they express themselves verbally or act different to the majority, they will feel heard, listened to, respected, and that they belong in the culture.

An individual or group should be fully present and mentally committed to the tasks at hand to do their job effectively. However, if we're having to hide how we're really feeling or show up at work as someone different than who we truly are, then this is what Kenji Yoshino (Chief Justice Earl Warren, professor of constitutional law at New York University School of Law) refers to as "covering."[40] This is a term used to describe not showing up as who you really are and instead adopting behaviours, language, attitudes, and traits the same as the majority groups around you so that you fit in. It is sometimes called "masking" and can refer to how neurodivergent people feel when conforming to neurotypical settings.

Sadly, the energy spent in maintaining a difference between the internal real self and the external projected persona has an emotional cost associated with it. This is a reality for how many people live their lives. **We need to strive for a culture where people can be fully in alignment externally and internally and feel psychologically safe in their own skin in their place of work.**

It's how we ensure people are mentally present and focused when doing their work, which is especially crucial in safety-critical roles in engineering. There are many high-hazard operations occurring daily and an underlying

---

[40] Kenji Yoshino, *Covering: The Hidden Assault on Our Civil Rights* (New York: Random House, 2007).

A NEW INCLUSIVE OPERATING SYSTEM 107

risk of loss of life if something goes wrong. Equally in low risk environments, mental health retains its power to kill.

There is an area within engineering called **Human Factors**, which looks at the working environment and how users respond in different scenarios.

Human factors refer to environmental, organisational, and job factors, and human and individual characteristics, which influence behaviour at work in a way that can affect Health & Safety.[41]

Human factors is concerned with what people are being asked to do (the task and its characteristics), who is doing it (the individual and their competence), and where they are working (the organisation and its attributes), all of which are influenced by the wider societal concern, both local and national.

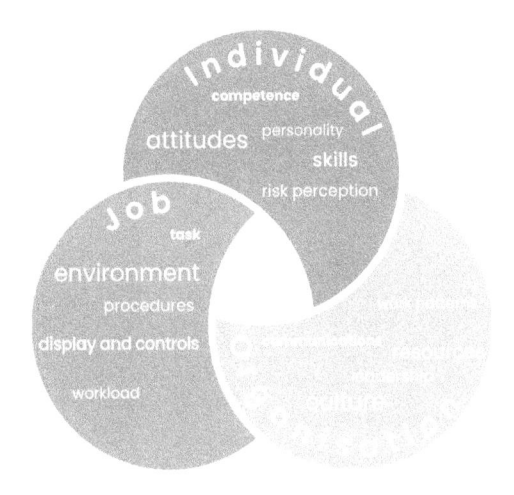

Figure 5.3. Human Factors in Occupational Health & Safety Venn Diagram

---

[41] "Reducing Error and Influencing Behaviour," Health & Safety Executive, https://www.hse.gov.uk/pubns/priced/hsg48.pdf.

A lot of thought goes into the user design of control rooms, production operations, and construction sites to maximise human response time in the event an alarm is sounded. For example, control room desks will automatically rise if an alarm is sounded, prompting control room operators to stand to attention and act.

So, with design innovations going into the ergonomics of how we do our engineering, what could we be doing regarding team culture forming?

Companies could offer mindful breakout spaces for people with anxiety; soundproof hubs for those with noise sensitivities; designated prayer rooms for people who need somewhere to pray during working hours every day; and desks that lower and rise for those with disabilities.

You can also look at the office layout to make sure there are no segregated areas or places more favourable to one group over another. If you have free drinks on a particular day, making sure you offer nonalcoholic alternatives creates an inclusive culture for those who don't drink for whatever reason. It even comes down to bathroom signage. Are they gender-neutral, or are gender-neutral options offered?

Little touches like these create an almost invisible inclusivity that doesn't force people to share their differences if they don't want to. It just normalises diversity and gives everyone the chance to experience and contribute to the team culture.

EqualEngineers has tools for performing human factors assessments to generate in-depth analyses for organisations to review, and benchmark their capability. It is beneficial to include some dedicated time for such assessments when performing design reviews for assets and operations.

Case Study

The following table showcases a typical analysis from a human factors (HF) assessment.[42]

UK HSE Top 10 HF Topics		Brief Description of Topic	Company 1	Company 2
1. Managing Human Factors	1.1 Human Factors in Risk Assessment	Structured inclusion of influences on human failure (violations and errors) in design and risk assessment		
	1.2 Incident Investigation	As above for incident investigation		
2. Procedures		Providing user-friendly procedures, which support error-free performance		
3. Training and Competence		Ability to undertake responsibilities and perform activities to a recognised standard on a regular basis; a combination of skills, experience, and knowledge		
4. Staffing	4.1 Staffing Levels	Right level of skilled people available for task		
	4.2 Workload	Manageable workload, especially during upsets and emergencies		

---

[42] "Getting Started," Human Factors 101, https://humanfactors101.com/getting-started/.

UK HSE Top 10 HF Topics		Brief Description of Topic	Company 1	Company 2
	4.3 Supervision	Experienced supervisors regularly present at work-site		
	4.4 Contractors	Competent contractors, properly supervised		
5. Organisational Change		Human aspects of organisational change risk assessed and controlled		
6. Safety-Critical Communications	6.1 Shift Handover	Structured process for shift and task handover in place and working as intended		
	6.2 Permit-To-Work	As above for permit-to-work		
7. Human Factors in Design	7.1 Control Rooms	Ergonomic design principles used		
	7.2 Human-Computer Interface	As above		
	7.3 Alarm Management	As above, to prevent alarm floods		
	7.4 Lighting, Thermal Comfort, Noise, and Vibration	As above		
8. Fatigue and Shiftwork		Work patterns designed to prevent/mitigate fatigue and reduce error		
9. Organisational and Safety Culture	9.1 Behavioural Safety	Programmes target critical behaviours and include process and occupational safety		

A NEW INCLUSIVE OPERATING SYSTEM 111

UK HSE Top 10 HF Topics		Brief Description of Topic	Company 1	Company 2
	9.2 Learning Organisations	Chronic unease exists, always looking for system causes of failure and opportunities to learn or improve		
10. Maintenance, Inspection and Testing	10.1 Maintenance Error	Structured process to minimise such errors in place – coupled with widespread awareness of risk of maintenance error		
	10.2 Intelligent Customers	The capability of the organisation to have a clear understanding of knowledge of the product or service being supplied; relevant to the use of contractors		

| RED | AMBER | GREEN |

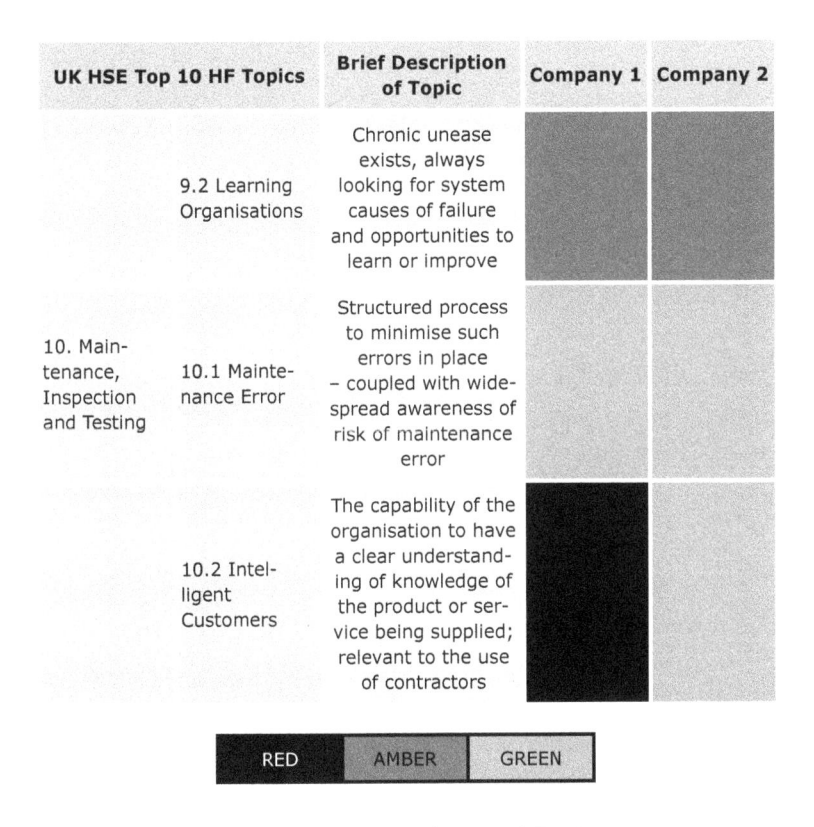

Figure 5.4. UK Health, Safety and Environment Top 10 Human Factors Topics table.

The Red/Amber/Green coding system helps guide how compliant an organisation is relevant to each topic.

DEI considerations need to be explicitly considered within the H&S/HF side of H&S management. For example, in the table, it contains Top 10 HF topics, and you can see that elements of them can relate to DEI situations:

- **Training and Competence (Topic 3):** Diversity in training and competence can refer to ensuring that educational materials and training programs are inclusive of different learning styles, languages, and cultural contexts. This includes making sure that all employees, regardless of their background, have equal access to training opportunities and are assessed fairly based on their abilities. It also involves recognising diverse competencies that individuals from various backgrounds bring to the table, which can enrich the collective skill set of the workforce.

- **Staffing Levels and Workload (Topic 4.1 and 4.2):** Equity and inclusion in staffing levels mean that decisions regarding recruitment, promotion, and retention practices should be free from bias, ensuring that all individuals have equal opportunities based on their merit. Workload management should also be equitable, preventing certain groups from being overburdened due to unconscious biases or systemic inequalities. This could be closely monitored through regular workload assessments and by promoting a culture that values diverse contributions equally.
- **Fatigue and Shift Work (Topic 8):** Fatigue and shift work can have a significant impact on mental health, contributing to stress, burnout, and in severe cases, mental ill-health and suicidal ideation. Companies must design work patterns that consider the mental well-being of their employees, providing adequate rest periods, and support for those on demanding schedules. Additionally, implementing programs that offer mental health education, creating an open dialogue about mental health issues, and providing access to support services can help mitigate these risks. Recognising and addressing the signs of mental health struggles early is crucial for preventing

them from escalating to more severe conditions like suicidal ideation.
- **Organisational and Safety Culture (Topic 9):** An inclusive organisational culture is critical for safety. Behavioral safety programs (Topic 9.1) should be designed to account for the diverse ways in which different groups perceive risks and respond to safety protocols. Learning organisations (Topic 9.2) should foster a culture where all employees feel safe to report incidents and suggest improvements, knowing their voices will be heard and valued regardless of their background. Chronic unease, as mentioned, should be a universal trait encouraged among all employees to proactively address safety concerns before they escalate.

These aspects help create an environment where all employees feel valued and able to contribute to their fullest potential, leading to improved safety outcomes, innovation, and overall organisational performance.

There is a risk that with a lack of representation, these assessments will not be as inclusive or wide reaching as they ought to be. They will be inherently limited by virtue of a narrow band of experience and cultures groups that are homogenous. This then perpetuates the issue of non-inclusive cultures.

Has a lack of diversity historically within high-hazard industries and engineering meant that we have created systems and processes that are inherently non-inclusive?

Concept: Stage 5 – Inclusive Interdependence©

This brings me back to what I propose as a new stage to the Bradley Curve, namely: **Stage 5: Inclusive Interdependence©**.

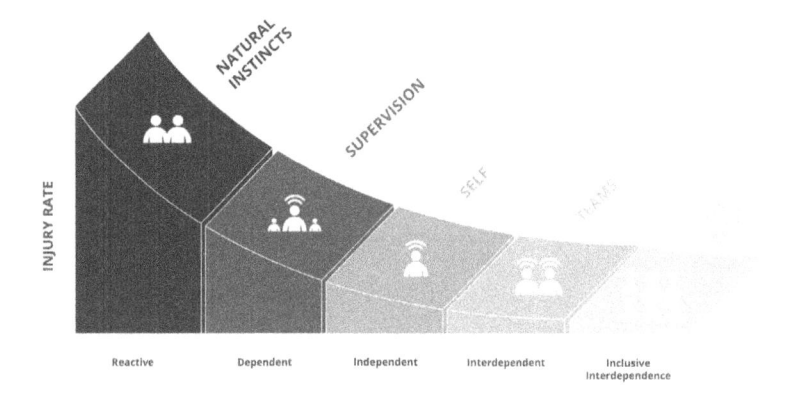

Figure 5.5. Stage 5 of Bradley Curve to include Inclusive Interdependence©.

In this stage, everyone recognises how looking out for the psychological safety of others is intrinsically beneficial *to themselves*. Collective accountability for ensuring psychological safety means that if you're looking out for the psychological safety and ensuring the positive wellbeing of someone else, then by reciprocity, others are also doing that *for you*.

The Allyship Paradox

The concept of allyship derives from LGBTQ+ networks talking about non-LGBTQ+ members being visibly supportive of creating inclusive cultures for LGBTQ+ communities. This has developed into allies showing their support by wearing rainbow-coloured lanyards, flying Pride flags in their offices, and/or attending pride parades with their company's LGBTQ+ employee network.

Recently, allyship has been more widely adopted to mean actively supporting any group to which you don't belong. There is an Inclusive Leader Continuum that illustrates moving from a position of: **Unaware > Aware > Active > Advocate**, developed by DEI thought-leader, Jennifer Brown.[43]

UNAWARE
You think diversity is compliance-related and simply tolerate it. It's someone else's job—not yours.

AWARE
You are aware that you have a role to play and are educating yourself about how best to move forward.

ACTIVE
You have shifted your priorities and are finding your voice as you begin to take meaningful action in support of others.

ADVOCATE
You are proactively and consistently confronting inequities and discrimination and working to bring about change in order to prevent them on a systemic level.

Private / Low Risk / Individual Perspective → Public / High Risk / Organisational Perspective

Figure 5.6. Inclusive Leader Continuum[44]

---

[43] Jennifer Brown, *How to Be an Inclusive Leader*, 2nd ed. (San Francisco: Berrett-Koehler Publishers, 2022).
[44] Brown, *Inclusive Leader*.

The implicit assumption with this model is that it requires a person who's curious and willing to learn about the needs and experiences of other groups different to their own. It requires them to expand their frame of reference on the world and learn secondarily. For example, watching videos online, reading interviews or books, listening to podcasts, attending events run by the employee network, or (dare I suggest it), just speaking to people!

Some people don't care, others don't have the time, and some won't make the effort. Some people have the intent but don't know how to act, and others are so tangled up by how they'll be received by another group that they never engage. Instead, they stay silent. Passive.

This concept of allyship requires the effort of the majority to work.

*This concept of **allyship** requires the effort of the majority to work*

It requires people to do something with no clearly articulated **direct** benefit to themselves (which goes back to our chimp brains). Some don't need this to motivate them; they're implicitly curious and want to create a better experience for the people around them. However, the more emphasis placed on how allyship is beneficial **for the individual engaging in it**, the more likely they are to do so.

An inherently inclusive culture with psychological safety embedded as a core tenet means that everyone knows it's pertinent to look out for the needs of their peers. This then shapes relationships and team dynamics for the better. Leadership styles of those who are in positions of power and who lead through power, fear, dominance, and control will then be challenged and weeded out. For those interested in learning more on the design concept of inherent safety design methods, please see the paper I coauthored for IChemE in 2015 at the Hazards 25 conference ("Inherent Safety: It's Common Sense, Now for Common Practice!").

If you would like to find out more about Inherently Inclusive Design assessments for your project or organisation, visit website by scanning QR code at the end of this chapter. You can also access the IChemE paper here as well.

Chapter six is going to focus on how H&S and DEI work together to build a team that sees the value in embedding psychological safety into their workplace.

Key Takeaways

- The Bradley Curve, conceptualised by Dr. H. James Bradley, outlines four stages that elucidate the causes of physical workplace incidents for preventive action.

- Redefining the Bradley Curve to include psychological safety offers a model for improving mental well-being at work.

- Human Factors (HF) engineering has the potential to integrate DEI elements into the design process.

- Allyship is pivotal in DEI but relies on widespread support; linking it to psychological safety can enhance engagement by showcasing its life-saving impact on mental health in engineering.

- Linking DEI to psychological safety can engage majority groups, addressing mental health issues in engineering.

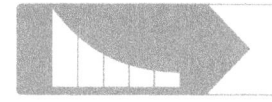

- Adding a 5th stage (Inclusive Interdependence) helps people recognise how looking out for the psychological safety of others is intrinsically beneficial to themselves.

Scan now and download the resources from this chapter.

Or visit:
equalengineers.com/TheSAFELeader/downloads

CHAPTER SIX

How Diversity, Equity, and Inclusion, and Health & Safety Interlink to Create Psychological Safety

Within the UK, organisations have an obligation under the **Health & Safety at Work Act 1974** to "ensure the health, safety, and welfare at work of all employees." This also applies to people on their premises, contractors, and any members of the public who may come into contact with their operations. Executive bonuses are often linked to safety performance – hence the constant scrutiny – and incidents are bad for a brand's reputation, which can take years to recover, if ever.

> **Case Studies: Health & Safety Fines**
>
> **Merlin Attractions Operations** paid the price in reputational damage and hefty fines when the theme park operator failed to stop two trains colliding on a ride at Alton Towers in 2015. This led to sixteen people being injured and one woman losing her leg. The incident resulted in a fine of between £5 million (due to the

company having a turnover in excess of £50 million).[45] This doesn't include the compensation the victims received. In fact, the victim who lost her leg received a multimillion pound settlement for her life-changing injuries.

Another example of reputational damage and financial repercussions was in 2016, when gas company **ConocoPhillips** was fined £3 million after a series of uncontrolled gas releases in their Lincolnshire offshore installation in 2012.[46] Although there were no casualties, due to the "high likelihood of serious injury or death" and the number of workers exposed to those risks, the fines were justified.

There is a big focus on occupational safety (tracking and reporting on slips, trips, and falls, etc.) in most workplaces, but what about health and well-being? As well as physical safety, the Health & Safety at Work Act (1974) has a requirement about people's mental health. **The law states that employers must try to remove or reduce stress "as far as is reasonably practical."**

So, how does DEI support H&S's mental health clause?

Like any relatively new concept, removing stress and creating a culture of well-being requires innovation. However,

---

[45] Stuart Mackie, "Record Fine for Alton Towers Health and Safety Failings," Thorntons Law, September 26, 2017, https://www.thorntons-law.co.uk/knowledge/record-fine-for-alton-towers-health-and-safety-failings.

[46] "ConocoPhillips (UK) Ltd v Health and Safety Executive (2016) Court of Appeal 23 December," Croner-i, April 3, 2017, https://app.croneri.co.uk/law-and-guidance/case-reports/conocophillips-uk-ltd-v-health-and-safety-executive-2016-court-appeal.

if those brainstorming sessions already feel difficult, try doing it without DEI.

The Groupthink Paradox

Groupthink is likely to occur when there is a lack of diversity in a group. Ideas are more likely to go unchallenged and risk poor-quality decision-making. Diverse teams comprise different demographics, life experiences, and perspectives, which all contribute to a design or operation that invariably leads to a better outcome (when teams are managed correctly).

I've seen highly capable technical professionals who've advanced into managerial posts but haven't been supported with the correct emotional intelligence skills training. As a baseline, managers should receive training on how to build inclusive teams and create a positive working environment for all. Training has a learning decay, so it's only a starting point, but people connect on a human-to-human level and inclusion enables this.

So, by investing in mechanisms that bring teams together, you're investing in creating a positive Health & Safety culture where people look out for one another. Mentoring and sponsoring can play a key role in cultivating organisational learning cultures and moments for people to develop deeper relationships than they readily will through the business-as-usual flow of work. As we have seen from the Trusted 10 exercise, organisations need to put in effort to create opportunity for interpersonal connection between people across different areas of the organisation to minimise bias and increase connection.

Merging H&S and DEI

DEI values every voice. H&S values every person.

DEI values
every **voice**

H&S values
every **person**

H&S policies aim to create a culture where people can call out issues when they see them without fear of recrimination. The goal is to drive constant improvements and share best practices. As DEI is proven to support healthier cultures, create empathy, and foster teams who look out for each other, the link is undeniable. **Better DEI = Better H&S**.

> **Case Study: Abdul's Story**
>
> Abdul works as an Artificial Intelligence (AI) engineer. He's teaching one of the machines to recognise discrimination, but it's not going well. His colleague, Sara, is on his team and working towards the same deadline.
>
> It's currently Ramadan and the company has loosely agreed to more flexible working for Abdul, although the pressures of deadlines means that he's still struggling to take the time he needs to look after himself. Because of this, the stress is mounting. Coupled with his fasting giving him brain fog, he's made some errors in judgement.

Sara has noticed the stress and understands why it's happening. She's asked for an extension on their deadline and the company has agreed to extend it by one week, despite the deadline still falling within the month of Ramadan. Sara notes this with Abdul, and between them, they agree to work to a different schedule. Sara will continue working how she is, and Abdul will work different hours so he's able to focus on his fasting without added stresses.

This goes a long way for Abdul feeling supported and less stressed, which is a huge cause of sickness leave. The project is completed within the new deadline, and both Sara and Abdul feel fairly treated and respected.

Names have been changed to protect identities.

People looking out for each other naturally results in a safer and more productive environment, as the Bradley Curve evidences. However, the more diversity of thought there is, the safer *everyone* becomes.

The **MORE** diversity of thought there is, the **SAFER** everyone becomes

This can be seen when women push for their average body metrics to be included when it comes to H&S standards, such as for PPE sizing. It can be seen when Muslim employees push for greater consideration during fasting periods like Ramadan. It can be seen when those on the autism spectrum request agile working solutions, and it can be seen when you create parity between mental health and physical health and sick days are reduced.

Using the Bradley Curve and my proposed **Stage 5: Inclusive Interdependence**© addition to the model, we can create teams that **link H&S and DEI to create an inclusive and psychologically safe environment**. This will result in happier teams, greater returns, and higher levels of productivity.

Psychological Safety Attracts Fresh Talent

Another way psychological safety improves teams is through attracting fresh talent. The conversation around mental health and well-being is becoming increasingly important to organisations and potential employees. Millennials and Gen Z – our current and future workforce – want to work for more diverse and inclusive companies where outdated stigmas surrounding mental health no longer exist.[47] And who knows how the collective value set of Generation Alpha and then Generation Beta are going to play out. We need to be ready to appeal as a sector in which people can thrive.

---

[47] Mahalia Mayne, "Constant Stress and Zero Tolerance of Toxic Workplaces: What Gen Z and Millennials Really Think About Work," People Management, November 30, 2023, https://www.peoplemanagement.co.uk/article/1849539/constant-stress-zero-tolerance-toxic-workplaces-gen-z-millennials-really-think-work.

And who knows how the collective value set of Generation α lpha and then Generation βeta are going to play out

In the engineering industry, and as the *Masculinity in Engineering* report shows us, the stigma of mental ill-health is still very much alive. Engineers are twice as likely to feel comfortable sharing their physical health problems as opposed to their mental health issues; over a third of engineers would describe their mental health as fair or poor, and over a fifth have had to take time off work because of it.[48]

A culture that updates its Operating System by merging H&S and DEI to create psychological safety within its workforce tackles this head-on, transforming the way people work and interact by putting their physical safety on par with their mental safety.

> **Case Study: Thames Water MHFAiders**[49]
>
> *"Mental health first-aiders are a catalyst for engagement, providing our employees with the confidence to come forward and seek support at their time of need."*
>
> Thames Water has revolutionised their mental health strategy to ensure it works for all employees, regardless

---

[48] McBride-Wright, "Masculinity in Engineering Research."
[49] Jane Cattermole, "Thames Water," MHFA England, https://mhfaengland.org/mhfa-centre/case-studies/thames-water/.

of their diversity. Their "Time to Talk" strategy employs mental health first-aiders, who are clearly defined by green lanyards that always represent their availability to talk. The success of this strategy is clear by the 75 percent reduction in referrals to Thames Water's Occupational Health Team for work-related stress, anxiety, and depression over the last five years.

Recommendations: How to Use DEI to Create an Inclusive H&S Culture

Understanding your work environment and ensuring everyone is represented equally or equitably, regardless of their diversity, means accidents are reduced and people feel supported.

Some examples include:

- Eradicating language barriers when it comes to hazard signs and no-access areas
- Offering religious accommodations like prayer rooms
- Having gender-neutral toilets or private changing rooms
- Acknowledgment of religious holidays or observances and accommodations put in place such as days off or flexible working
- Flexible or agile working for parents and carers

Difficult Questions to Ask Ourselves
Do men, women, trans, and nonbinary people have equal H&S needs?
Are non-English speakers more likely to be put at risk?
Are LGBTQIA+ people out and comfortable on site?
Are neurodivergent individuals given time and space to express their views or give feedback?
Are disabled people empowered to reveal their disabilities?

Sickness policies and procedures tend to monitor stress leave through occupational health referrals, but they're essentially an organisational tick box exercise with no real benefit to the person attending the appointment (other than an assurance they won't lose their job). To support and improve a workforce's mental health, there needs to be a conversation about it first.

This comes down to four key approaches:

- **Stage one:** Implementing a robust DEI strategy and linking it to H&S to create psychological safety
- **Stage two:** Introducing innovative training initiatives and refresher sessions
- **Stage three:** Connecting humans with humans through empathetic learning
- **Stage four:** Nurturing a workforce culture in which people look out for each other

> **Mental Health vs. Diversity Statistics: The Prince's Responsible Business Network**[50]
>
> When it comes to gender, 66 percent of women are more likely to report experiencing poor mental health at work, while 37 percent of men are reluctant to discuss mental health problems with anyone at work.
>
> When it comes to ethnicity, 25 percent of nonwhite employees stated their ethnicity was a factor in their mental health symptoms caused by work, compared to 1 percent of those who were white. Additionally, 25 percent of ethnic minority managers cited having no resources or materials for support, compared to 14 percent of white managers.
>
> When it comes to disability, 52 percent of disabled employees have been diagnosed with a mental health condition, compared to 25 percent without a disability. Furthermore, 38 percent of those with a disability are more likely to feel that their organisations don't do enough to support them.
>
> When it comes to LGBTQIA+, 79 percent of people are likely to have experienced poor mental health where work was a cause or contributing factor, compared to 60 percent of heterosexual employees.

From these statistics, it's clear why organisations with a successful DEI strategy – one that fosters inclusion and support of all individuals – would have happier and more productive teams. These figures make it clear that *inclusive* Health & Safety is needed to better support diverse

---

[50] "Mental Health at Work 2019: Time to Take Ownership," Business in the Community, https://www.bitc.org.uk/report/mental-health-at-work-2019-time-to-take-ownership/.

individuals. If we aren't willing to fix the problem, we remain a part of the issue.

Bowtie diagrams are used in safety engineering to communicate the causes and consequences of major hazards.

It has long stood as a cornerstone tool, illustrating the multifaceted nature of risk management and barrier implementation. Traditionally, these diagrams serve to visually dissect and understand the complex interplay between potential hazards and the controls in place to mitigate them.

However, we've taken a bold step in repurposing this powerful tool, applying its principles to breaking down barriers faced by underrepresented groups in the engineering sector to create DEI Bowtie Diagrams©. This innovative approach not only illuminates the challenges these groups encounter but also offers a structured pathway to dismantle these obstacles, fostering a more inclusive and equitable work environment.

We use these as a workshop engagement tool to delve into the intricacies of barriers that often go unseen and unaddressed. These barriers, ranging from subtle biases to systemic hindrances, impede the growth and participation of diverse talents in engineering. We have created a vivid and interactive workshop tool, empowering employees to engage actively with these issues. This is a tool framing the language of DEI in a language understood by majority-group engineers working in high risk environments.

The diagram acts as a mirror, reflecting both the current state of inclusivity within your organisation and the potential routes to cultivate a more diverse and supportive workplace. This hands-on approach encourages not just awareness but active participation in crafting solutions, turning passive observers into change agents.

Our journey with this adapted Bowtie diagram is more than just a workshop exercise; it's a commitment to transformation. We invite you to explore these diagrams not just as tools of understanding, but as blueprints for action.

Each barrier identified is a call to action, each mitigating control a step towards progress. DEI should be celebrated and leveraged for greater innovation and success.

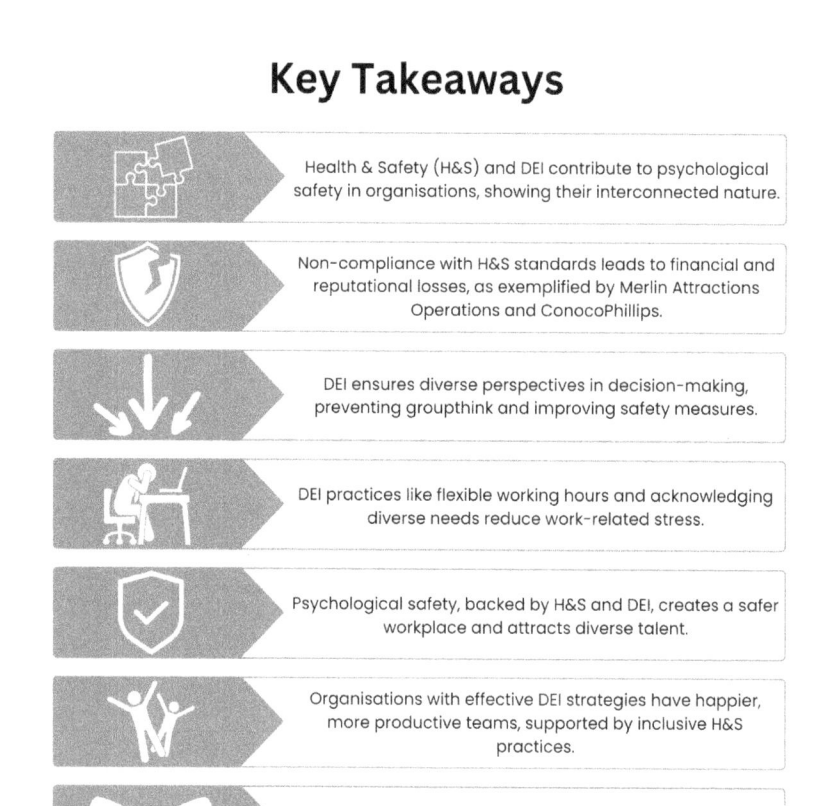

Key Takeaways

- Health & Safety (H&S) and DEI contribute to psychological safety in organisations, showing their interconnected nature.

- Non-compliance with H&S standards leads to financial and reputational losses, as exemplified by Merlin Attractions Operations and ConocoPhillips.

- DEI ensures diverse perspectives in decision-making, preventing groupthink and improving safety measures.

- DEI practices like flexible working hours and acknowledging diverse needs reduce work-related stress.

- Psychological safety, backed by H&S and DEI, creates a safer workplace and attracts diverse talent.

- Organisations with effective DEI strategies have happier, more productive teams, supported by inclusive H&S practices.

- Innovative tools like DEI Bowtie Diagrams© identify barriers to inclusion, engaging employees in promoting equity.

Scan now and download the resources from this chapter.

Or visit:
equalengineers.com/TheSAFELeader/downloads

CHAPTER SEVEN

Engaging the Majority: Masculinity in Engineering

We've already talked about the benefits of DEI, how it extends and merges with H&S to create psychological safety, and how to approach embedding a strategy within your organisation. However, we haven't looked at the biggest barrier to implementing this in male-majority teams – especially where they feel blamed for the existence of DEI initiatives in the first place. The barrier in question is the lack of engagement of men in DEI strategy. We need to drive active participation from the group that makes up the largest percentage of the current engineering workforce. This chapter suggests ways to engage the male majority through the "I" in DEI: **inclusion**.

It's important to understand this isn't about taking anything away from hard-won safe spaces for equality and diversity within the workforce. However, for a truly psychologically safe workforce, everyone in it needs to be on board with creating the same culture change. Otherwise, you risk your investment in DEI failing and will miss out on the benefits of inclusive, innovative, and productive teams.

One way to include the male majority in the conversation around DEI is to empathetically engage them with their own diversity story. One of the most available and most important doors to open for them is the discussion around their mental health and the pressures and expectations placed on them by society.

We all have a brain and we all have feelings (regardless of whether we acknowledge them!) and the discussion around mental health is a shared experience everyone on the planet has a right to weigh in on.

Men's Engagement

Our *Masculinity in Engineering* study recommended a greater focus on the "health" in Health & Safety. The findings also supported **the Health & Safety at Work Act's** recommendation that companies need to consider their employees' mental health and well-being too. Many companies believe they're covered if they offer a well-being app and/or occupational health referral schemes. However, these initiatives are merely plasters on wounds that require a more robust response.

Engineering and technology in the UK and USA are predominantly male-dominated professions. Men comprise over 84 percent of the workforce. Statistics show how engineering has a problem with mental ill-health. Our profession is losing people to suicide, while men are 3.5 times more likely than women to say they've self-harmed or considered taking their own lives.

Some solutions to overcome this would be to destigmatise talking openly about mental ill-health, encourage more leaders to speak openly about their personal struggles to humanise it, and promote an organisational culture that embodies healthy masculinity.

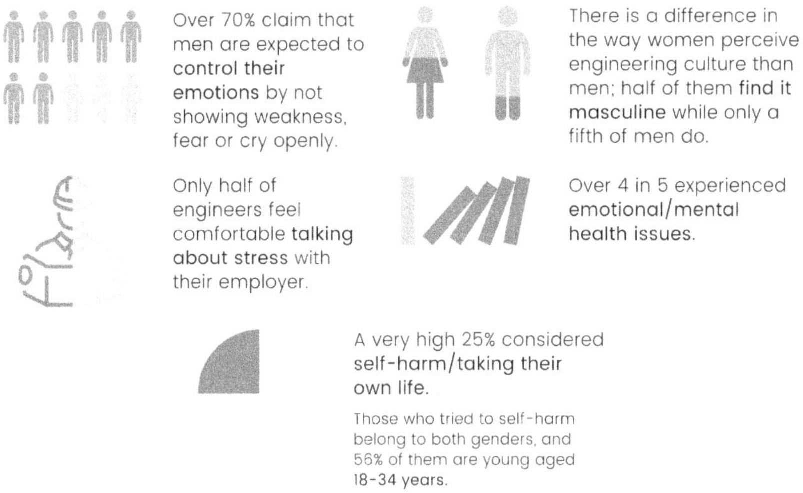

ENGAGING THE MAJORITY: MASCULINITY IN ENGINEERING   135

Over 70% claim that men are expected to control their emotions by not showing weakness, fear or cry openly.

There is a difference in the way women perceive engineering culture than men; half of them find it masculine while only a fifth of men do.

Only half of engineers feel comfortable talking about stress with their employer.

Over 4 in 5 experienced emotional/mental health issues.

A very high 25% considered self-harm/taking their own life.

Those who tried to self-harm belong to both genders, and 56% of them are young aged 18-34 years.

Figure 7.1. Key Findings from 2022 *Masculinity in Engineering* Research:[51]

- Over 70 percent claim that men are expected to control their emotions by not showing weakness, fear, or crying openly.
- Women perceive engineering culture different than men; half of them find it masculine while only a fifth of men do.
- Only 50 percent of engineers feel comfortable talking about stress with their employer.
- Over four in five experienced emotional/mental health issues.
- A very high percentage (25 percent) considered self-harm / taking their own life.
- Those who tried to self-harm belong to both genders, and 56 percent of them are young, aged eighteen to thirty-four years.

---

[51] McBride-Wright, "Masculinity in Engineering Research."

These statistics are concerning and shape my belief about the need for a culture shift. Creating psychological safety by using the lessons from successful DEI campaigns and merging them with inclusive H&S will save lives. The benefit of helping men share their own diversity story and/or struggles with mental health is twofold:

- It will help them relate to others with their own struggles
- It will help them express themselves free from bias and stigma

This is doubly important when you consider how only 31 percent of engineers feel included in the environment they work in. Six in ten feel alienated by the existing masculine culture, and less than a quarter of engineers would feel comfortable discussing their challenges battling depression or financial stress with colleagues or their superiors.[52]

> I think many men are used to dwelling in loss by themselves instead of letting someone else comfort them.
>
> – Masculinity in Engineering report 2019

If we don't create human-centred cultures where the brain is considered as important as the body, we remain in an outdated Operating System. If we

---
[52] McBride-Wright, "Masculinity in Engineering Research."

operate in a redundant space, we're not evolving alongside a globalised and emotionally aware world. The engineering industry needs to step up and embrace these changes if it doesn't want to be left behind.

Men as Allies

In the book *Showing Up: How Men Can Become Effective Allies in the Workplace*, Ray Arata dives deep into the themes of masculinity and the various ways men can become better allies in their respective workplaces.[53]

By analysing both traditional and modern notions of masculinity, Arata provides a comprehensive set of insights for male readers looking to make an impact in their respective jobs.

The main theme of the book is that men can become more effective allies by stepping outside of traditional masculine stereotypes and learning to recognise existing gender biases within the workplace.

Men have a responsibility to break away from "manly" tropes and show up as better allies to those around them. I encourage men to become conscious of the power and privilege they hold by virtue of their sex, and to use it as a force for making the world a better place.

As men, we need to firstly become aware of our own biases and behaviours and how we view ourselves in relation to what it stereotypically means to be a man. What impact has our upbringing had on us? Who were our male role models? And was it a healthy portrayal of

---

[53] Ray Arata, *Showing Up: How Men Can Become Effective Allies in the Workplace* (New York: Diversion Books, 2022).

masculinity? The context within which we were raised has become our emotional, subconscious reference point for how we show up today, both in our personal and professional lives. Often we have not had a whole range of emotions shown to us. Our go-to emotional reaction is anger.

This is what has traditionally been modeled in society as the image of a successful male. Powerful, dominant, aggressive, and where showing any vulnerability, let alone crying, is out of the question. "Man up" has become a phrase for a reason.

Therefore, for men especially, the first stage of the work starts with us. Internal self-reflection to understand our own diversity story. What adversity have we been through? What emotional ghosts from the past have we buried and not explored? What emotions/experiences do we have unreconciled that are potentially the undercurrent of our surface reactions? We have a lot of collective unpacked emotional baggage and are moving through this world with the expectations still bestowed upon us of what men ought to do: provide for our family, be the primary earner, be strong, and have it all together, all of the time. Times are changing, and we need to recast what it means to be a man in the twenty-first century and then use our position of power and privilege to platform the experiences of others who have compounded inequity stacked against them because of intersectional identities.

By being mindful of attitudes and behaviours that in practice are sexist or oppressive towards women, men are able to develop empathy towards other genders in the workplace. Arata emphasises that men should take responsibility for their actions and be willing to learn from their mistakes in order to create more equitable workplaces. Men can support their colleagues from minoritised groups through mentorship opportunities, actively listening, and understanding gender dynamics.

Start an internal men's network to help coalesce people who are interested in connecting on topics related to men's health and well-being. EqualEngineers has a cross-sector men's network for people interested in joining a community outside of their workplace. Visit equalengineers.com for more information.

Organise a retreat/offsite with other likeminded men who are interested in finding a new way in their lives. There is a growing movement within men's work to tackle self-sabotage and learn how to be a better man. Contact EqualEngineers if you are interested in learning more.

How to Embed DEI in Male-Majority Teams and Save Lives

When it comes to embedding DEI in male-majority teams, success depends on two factors: leadership and training. There's no one-size-fits-all approach, but there are several tried and tested techniques that have proven to yield positive outcomes.

Inclusive Leadership

> **"An inclusive leader is someone who has a strong self-awareness about their own preferred work style but is able to flex this style to connect with all of their team, even those who think and work differently and who may have totally different motivators."**
>
> – *Charlotte Sweeney OBE and Fleur Bothwick OBE, Inclusive Leadership*

SAFE Leaders set the tone from the top. As a result, they're the catalysts for successful DEI strategies. A SAFE Leader is committed to diversity and inclusion because this forms a part of their value system; they believe in the business case for diversity. However, despite being uniquely placed to model change and influence a collective, many leaders are scared about how they'll be perceived. Breaking free of those mental restrictions requires a mindset shift.

The mental restrictions leaders often face when discussing diversity and inclusion may include:

1. **Fear of misspeaking:** Many leaders may worry about the possibility of inadvertently causing offence, leading to a hesitant approach to DEI discussions.
2. **Misunderstanding and lack of knowledge:** Leaders may not fully grasp the dynamics and challenges faced by different diversity groups, resulting in a fear of engaging in discussions they feel ill-prepared for.
3. **Concern over authenticity:** Some leaders may feel that advocating for diversity and inclusion is perceived as a corporate requirement rather than a personally important cause, leading to concern over how genuine their efforts may seem.
4. **Fear of change:** Diversifying teams and implementing DEI strategies often means changing traditional systems and dynamics, which can be daunting.
5. **Resistance to vulnerability:** Discussing issues of diversity and inclusion often requires admitting personal blind spots and biases, which necessitates a level of vulnerability some leaders may be uncomfortable with.

Here are five things to consider in shifting your mindset to become a SAFE Leader:

1. **Practice active listening:** Effective communication is key. SAFE Leaders should strive to listen to understand, not to respond, thereby promoting respectful conversations about DEI.
2. **Adopt a learning mindset:** SAFE Leaders should be open to learning about different diversity groups, their unique experiences, and their challenges. This mindset will help to dismantle fear and misconceptions and will show team members that it's okay to learn and grow.
3. **Be proactive in seeking feedback:** SAFE Leaders should encourage others to give them feedback on their DEI efforts and be open to constructive criticism. This not only helps leaders improve, but also fosters a culture of openness, respect, and continuous improvement.
4. **Believe in the power of diversity:** SAFE Leaders should internalise the understanding that diversity isn't just a tick box for corporate social responsibility but a strategic business advantage. Diversity brings a variety of perspectives, which can drive innovation and decision-making.
5. **Embrace vulnerability:** SAFE Leaders can set a powerful example by admitting what they don't know and asking for help. This can foster a culture of openness and honesty, encouraging everyone in the organisation to do the same.

People experience who you are by what you share and stand up for. If you're a leader in an organisation, you're a mini-celebrity with uniquely placed power over its culture. The leadership shadow you cast carries more emotional weight when you're able to share your vulnerability and dimensions.

People do not trust robots with no emotional overlays. Engineering culture is almost universally seen as problem-solving, while only 20 percent of engineers consider it personable (where they're able to talk about personal matters), which is very low.[54] Engineers are more comfortable dealing with things than people, but people need to be dealt with as people and not things.

There are many parallels between a positive **safety** culture and a positive **inclusive** culture, which both require the same commitment from senior leaders. However, the latter is often misunderstood or deemed less relevant to the core of the business. It's not tackled with the same ferocity as safety. Perhaps this is because executive bonuses are linked to safety Key Performance Indicators and not to organisational diversity.

Self-Development

Leaders should take the opportunity to enrol in reciprocal mentoring relationships where they are paired with an engineering student currently studying at university, or an engineering apprentice working at the early stages of their career, or perhaps a returner who has recently returned to the workplace after an extended period of absence from the profession. Ideally mentoring relationships will be with someone with different diversity demographics too to offer the opportunity for lived experience knowledge exchange. Check out the EqualEngineers Pathways Programme for more information.

---

[54] McBride-Wright, "Masculinity in Engineering Research."

To further support learning, I have been increasingly getting asked to coach senior leaders who feel that they have no one to turn to when it comes to leading their organisation through what can feel quite a daunting, transformational change. They are simply scared of saying the wrong thing, and want a place where they can offload, ask the questions they are afraid of asking, and run through scenarios. When you are at the healm of an organisation, the stakeholders around you can have implicit biases, filter information, or be inherently not-neutral, given that they may be in your reporting line. Therefore as a SAFE Leader, it is worth investing in external coaching to have someone you can share information with confidentially and troubleshoot how you might deal with situations you find yourself in.

If we're serious about creating an inclusive profession, we need to get more disruptive with the way we tackle the issues. To become SAFE Leaders, all leaders in engineering:

1. Need to go through baseline training on this new culture change model;
2. Should consistently have a reciprocal mentoring relationship on the go with an upcoming engineering student so that they remain grounded to the future talent; and
3. Should have a personal learning space/community where they can share their fears and have the support they need to hone how they show up.

Recognising DEI is People-Led

It helps if we look at diversity in the same way we look at biodiversity. In nature, diversity is essential for the ecosystem.

In the workforce, diversity generates revenue and repeat business due to how various ideas interact, the multiple angles considered, and the final solution that has gone through a robust and diverse process. It also lends itself to appealing to a more diverse customer and client base.

That said, all the new ideas, creativity, and innovation aren't worth anything if those contributions and perspectives aren't being listened to and valued, which is why the proper implementation of a DEI strategy is key. And when it forms part of an inclusive H&S strategy, led by SAFE Leaders, it is likelier to get embedded within business-as-usual work practice.

Embedding DEI in an organisation requires everyone to recognise their identities and intersectionality. How people's identities intersect can encourage empathetic learning. DEI fails because of a lack of engagement. So, to truly embed DEI in the workforce, everyone needs to be on board, and this can only happen when organisations focus on the "inclusive" in DEI.

It's about looking at the great work of diversity groups and applying those same strategies to the whole organisation. It's about including the male majority in the conversation, focussing on the "toxic" in toxic masculinity, and allowing men to talk about how it harms them too. This is not about taking away sorely fought for employee network groups; it's about opening up the workplace culture such that those with higher suicidal ideation can benefit from destigmatisation.

So, how is this done?

Embedding DEI in organisations starts with SAFE Leaders setting the tone. Leaders should care and embody the values of inclusion, such as curiosity, cultural intelligence, collaboration, commitment, courage, and cognisance. It shouldn't be done as a token gesture. It should be done because it's the right thing to do – not just for the entire workforce, but the whole organisation: from stakeholder engagement to profits, marketing to innovation, and social responsibility to parity.

> Getting started on this work can feel overwhelming, and in order for it to be done effectively, it requires specialists to help facilitate the process, similar to how the H&S department functions within an organisation. Why not employ a DEI specialist to come and train your staff? Companies such as EqualEngineers are on a mission to unlock the power of diversity and inclusion for greater company culture and performance, so be sure to look for training that aligns with your vision and morals and pick one that will help you reach your DEI goals productively and sustainably.

Part of ensuring that happens comes down to the way we treat employees, their diversity, and their mental health.

This comes back to the fact that DEI and H&S are people-led. The entire workforce should be involved in making a DEI strategy successful – from interns to CEOs. No one should be left behind. It should permeate and adapt, which can only happen when organisations take the time to understand their workforce and encourage discussion.

Once this is achieved, the organisation can – and will – benefit from the unique talent on offer, as well as the new ideas and revenue a diverse workforce generates.

The age of globalisation has changed the way we do business, and because of that, our organisations need to change and adapt too, updating to an Inclusive Operating

System.© To be competitive within your chosen market not only depends on the amount of innovation and creativity being cultivated but on how engaged, valued, and supported our workforces are.

Managing Diversity

A diversified workforce can pose unique challenges for management. Having similarities and differences among employees regarding their age, cultural background, physical abilities, neuro-capabilities, race, religion, gender, and sexual identity can be tricky to navigate. However, when managed and implemented properly, DEI becomes an undisputed organisational strength.

> **D**iversity, **E**quity and **I**nclusion becomes an undisputed organisational strength

This strength will permeate the entire workforce. Employees who work for companies that value, listen, and encourage their staff are more likely to work harder – efficiency being a key component for productivity. Creating a culture of inclusion means staff enjoy coming to their place of work and are more invested in its success.

Collaborating with supply chain partners is another way to ensure collective accountability and a focus on doing better. Putting in requirements in procurement policies and procedures for tender replies is a way to ensure your supply chain partners will make DEI a priority focus area.

ENGAGING THE MAJORITY: MASCULINITY IN ENGINEERING   147

It's important to note that there isn't a one-size-fits-all approach when it comes to implementing and managing your DEI strategy. It will depend on the needs of your organisation. However, there are various tools available that will help you update your Operating System to enable psychological safety in your workforce.

There are several training programmes that have been designed to help organisations better manage components that we have discussed throughout this book.

Bystander Training

We might call out the negative behaviour of the perpetrator and check that the victim is okay. This is usually better done in a group setting.

Direct — We might speak to the victim and offer them a reason for them to leave the situation, such as taking a pretend call or having a conversation with them ourselves.

Distract

Delay — We might wait for the situation to pass if we deem it too dangerous to intervene, then ask the victim if they're okay. We might report the incident and/or call the police.

When we delegate, we might ask others to intervene and support us or call for help by involving the authorities straight away.

Delegate

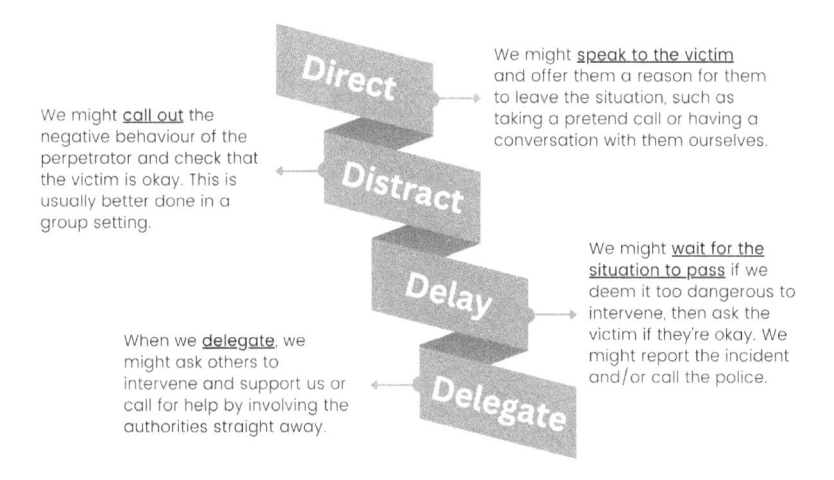

Figure 7.2. 4D's Model Framework.

When someone has been in an incident which has led to a physical injury, first responders helping the individual usually deploy basics of first-aid training. If they are unconscious, this involves Airway-Breathing-Circulation (ABC). Even if we are not first-aid trained, we instinctively know that we need to get help.

People who are trained learn models and frameworks so that they can launch straight into action if it ever becomes needed. This is because as time ticks by, the person's likelihood of recovery diminishes.

Bystander training provides a model for you to intervene to address issues around bullying, harassment, microaggressions, and microinequities. These are things that put psychological safety at risk.

Bystander intervention is an approach that can be used to improve situations where it looks like someone could use some help. The approach is about being an active, positive contributor, instead of ignoring the situation or expecting someone else to step in and fix it.

Bystanders are witnesses who have seen something bad happen. This could apply in the workplace context, or even in your personal life or whilst travelling around. Passive bystanders are people who choose, for whatever reason, to ignore the situation or to do nothing about it. Active bystanders are people who do something to try to improve the situation. People may be reluctant or hesitate to become an active bystander in the moment when it is needed because they do not know what to do or how to respond.

When bystanders see or hear something that makes them think *somebody should do something about this,* passive bystanders think *somebody else should do something about this* and active bystanders think *I should do something about this*. This is where Inclusive Interdependence© motivates the passive bystander to take action because even though morally it is the right thing to do, there is something in it for them.

The 4D model provides a framework to call upon to consider how am I going to handle this situation.

- Direct Action
- Distract
- Delay
- Delegate

When we challenge unacceptable behaviours, we tend to do so in four ways: through direct action, distraction, delaying tactics, or delegation. For example, if we're on a train and witness a racially motivated verbal attack on a woman, we'll either respond by ignoring it and deciding it isn't our problem or doing one of the following:

Distract: We might speak to the victim and offer them a reason for them to leave the situation, such as taking a pretend call or having a conversation with them ourselves so they don't have to acknowledge the perpetrator.

Direct action: We might call out the negative behaviour of the perpetrator and check that the victim is okay. This is usually better done in a group setting.

Delay: We might wait for the situation to pass if we deem it too dangerous to intervene, then ask the victim if they're okay. We might report the incident and/or call the police.

Delegate: When we delegate, we might ask others to intervene and support us or call for help by involving the authorities straight away.

There is also a 6D version of this model if you wish to take it a step further with "Document" and "Defend". If other forms of intervention aren't possible, you can record the situation by taking a picture or video. If possible, make sure you have consent of the harmed party before sharing this documentation.

Direct — We might **speak to the victim** and offer them a reason for them to leave the situation, such as taking a pretend call or having a conversation with them ourselves.

Distract — We might **call out** the negative behaviour of the perpetrator and check that the victim is okay. This is usually better done in a group setting.

Delay — We might **wait for the situation to pass** if we deem it too dangerous to intervene, then ask the victim if they're okay. We might report the incident and/or call the police.

Delegate — When we **delegate**, we might ask others to intervene and support us or call for help by involving the authorities straight away.

Document — You can **record the situation** by taking a picture or video. If possible, make sure you have consent of the harmed party before sharing this documentation.

Defend — If can be difficult to be the courageous individual being the first to intervene in a problematic situation. However, if you do see someone stepping in, **back them up**. Position yourself close to them so they know they have support.

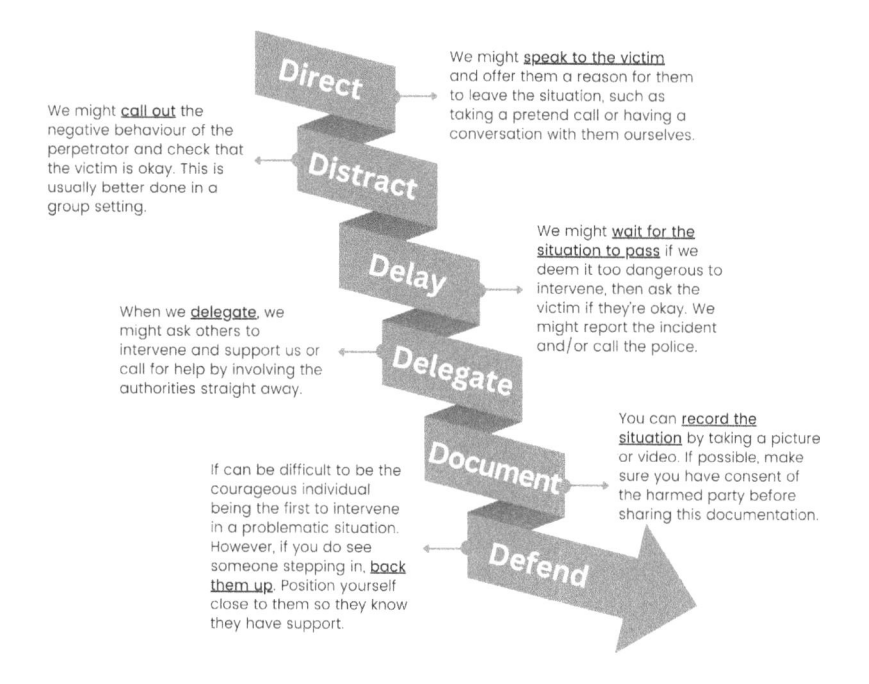

Figure 7.3. 6D's Model Framework.

If can be difficult to be the courageous individual being the first to intervene in a problematic situation. However, if you do see someone stepping in, back them up. Position yourself close to them so they know they have support. Piggyback off of their intervention. Even if it looks like the situation is under control, be observant and ready if needed.

Bystander training is about breaking the silence of inaction and empowering people to act when they see harmful behaviours. It teaches people to assess situations accordingly and ensure the best safety outcomes for themselves and the victim.

By overcoming the fear paralysis in confrontational situations and using the right words and techniques to achieve positive safety outcomes, we empower ourselves and the victims we're standing up for while disempowering the perpetrators engaging in harmful behaviours.

Bystander training also teaches people how to tackle microinequities, such as eye rolls and sighs, and talks about unconscious bias and how to fight it. In that regard, it's an evolution of unconscious bias training that helps encourage action *and* thought (instead of thought alone).

ALGEE Training

Another useful training tool originates from the charity **Mental Health First Aid**, which uses the acronym ALGEE to teach practitioners how to perform mental health first aid. It encourages people to:

1. **A**ssess risk
2. **L**isten nonjudgmentally
3. **G**ive reassurance and information
4. **E**ncourage appropriate professional help
5. **E**ncourage self-help and other support strategies

Over 2.5 million people are certified MHFAs and use the ALGEE action plan to shape their responses to people's mental health.[55] However, just like how first-aiders are not qualified doctors, MHFAs are not psychologists. They're a precautionary measure – a first responder in the

---

[55] "ALGEE: How MHFA Helps You Respond in Crisis and Non-Crisis Situations," Mental Health First Aid, April 15, 2021, https://www.mentalhealthfirstaid.org/2021/04/algee-how-mhfa-helps-you-respond-in-crisis-and-non-crisis-situations/.

workplace – and they are there to offer support, not diagnose, an individual's mental health.

ASIST Training

A useful training to also consider is Applied Suicide Intervention Skills Training (ASIST). It is a two-day interactive workshop in suicide first aid. ASIST training equips individuals with the skills to become more alert to the signs of suicidal thoughts and understand the various factors that may contribute to someone's distress.

Trainees learn to recognise when someone might be asking for help and the barriers they face in seeking support. The program emphasises the importance of practicing guidance and providing tailored suicide first aid, aimed at addressing the unique safety needs of the person at risk.

Participants also learn to develop and implement effective suicide safety plans, while appreciating the critical role of community resources and support networks in suicide prevention. Additionally, ASIST training underscores the significance of life-promotion and the necessity of self-care for those involved in this vital work.

This is training that all organisations should be investing in for their people, and especially organisations in engineering.

Case Study

EqualEngineers secured funding from the Engineering Construction Industry Training Board (ECITB) to deliver training to over 1,000 engineers in the UK nuclear sector. This training was curated specifically for this sector, fusing in insights from our *Masculinity in Engineering* report to create our "Engineering Inclusive Cultures: Engaging the Majority" training course. This was completed virtually following the impact of the Covid-19 pandemic and it enabled difficult conversations to be had. Overall, learners reported a signicant improvement in their understanding of DEI, the role they can play in being an active ally, and how mental health and well-being in respect of the experience of the male majority can be used as a tool to engage people on the need for inclusive cultures.

These are just some revolutionary tools for helping you embed DEI in your organisation. EqualEngineers assesses each business before working with them, pinpointing key areas of improvement and offering advice and training on tackling these aspects for a higher chance of DEI implementation success. Training is only one piece of the diversity pie; ongoing refresher sessions and deep organisational shifts are needed to avoid training decay. To find out how we could help your organisation, visit equalengineers.com/contact to get in touch.

Key Takeaways

- The prevalence of mental health issues among men, particularly in the male-dominated engineering sector, is increasingly concerning.

- Inclusion-centered DEI allows the male majority to engage with initiatives that enhance well-being without diminishing the value of existing DEI spaces.

- A comprehensive DEI strategy engages the majority through inclusive leadership, mental health literacy, and empathy, fostering a shared mental health experience.

- Establish networks focusing on various identities, including a men's network, to address and learn from the impacts of unhealthy masculinity within the organisation.

- Personability in leadership, emphasising inclusivity and shared learning, is vital for SAFE Leaders to build trust and inspire team openness.

- Foster DEI integration by collaborating with supply chains to make it a standard practice and a weighted factor in contractual agreements.

- DEI success hinges on universal empowerment within the workforce, ensuring it transcends mere formalities to achieve genuine benefits.

- Tools like SAFE Leader and SHIELD frameworks, DEI Bowtie workshops, and Bystander training support discussions on DEI and psychological safety in the workplace.

Scan now and download the resources from this chapter.

Or visit:
equalengineers.com/TheSAFELeader/downloads

CONCLUSION

The Future of Engineering: A System that Works for *ALL*!

> Creating an organisation that values its workforce is the same as creating a workforce that values its organisation.
>
> – Dr. Mark McBride-Wright, MBE, CEng, MIChemE

And it is not just professional, it is also personal. I am a father, and my husband and I have two children. Our son, Hunter, is four, and our daughter, Willow, is two. And we play a little game at bathtime. Bathtime in our house is at 6:30 p.m. We get the kids out of the bath, I wrap my son up in a towel, and I take him through to his bedroom. Now, before he gets his pyjamas on and we blow dry his hair and read a story, the game we have to play is the Hungry Caterpillar, based on the children's book which you may have read growing up. What we have to do is Hunter curls up in a ball all nice and tight on the floor, and then I have to take the towel and place it over him. I then have to narrate the story:

> "One day, there was a very hungry caterpillar who ate one apple . . . two bananas . . . three oranges . . . four strawberries . . . five raspberries. . ."
>
> Hunter (muffled): "Dada – you forgot the cake!"
>
> "Oh, sorry, Hunter. And one piece of cake. The caterpillar was full, until he had one piece of lettuce to settle his tummy. He wraps himself up tight into a cocoon for a few weeks."

Hunter then pulls the towel in closer to himself, and then he starts to wiggle, he starts to shake. And then the caterpillar bursts out of the cocoon, and with that movement, Hunter takes the towel off and throws it aside. He comes out and then flaps his wings like a beautiful butterfly around the bedroom. He is free.

And I see the way in this world that we start to box young four-year-old boys into what we expect them to be. Limiting self-expression and not letting them show up fully. I am sure we have all, at some point in our lives, experienced feeling confined, shackled, constrained. I invite you to consider that if you are ever feeling like this, all you have to do is:

- Share
- Hear
- Act
- Kindness
- Empathy

SHAKE©!

Figure 8.1. SHAKE© Model.

This model can be applied in any situations where you feel like the world is closing in on you. When you feel like your voice is not being heard. It starts with being honest within ourselves. Sharing what we are really feeling personally, verbalising it, and hearing ourselves.

Aches and pains are our bodies' way of telling us something is wrong, and it's important to be attuned to what they are trying to tell us.

And taking action should we need to get any professional help if the thoughts are becoming damaging.

It's important to be kind to ourselves and give ourselves space to adapt, adjust, and settle into any new changes in our lives, or traumatic experiences.

And having empathy for those who may be going through similar experiences but to whom we have never connected with.

We can also apply this model to how we connect with others. Create space for people to share and speak their truth. Tune in to what they are saying and actively listen. Don't listen with the intention to respond, but focus and tune-out the inner monologue in your head. Observe as well the nonverbal communication, the body language, and what is **not** being said as well as what **is** being said.

How we respond to whatever is being shared can affect what the individual does next, or their subsequent recovery. Showing kindness and empathy goes a long way to helping ameliorate a situation and get them to a better place. It can help you truly understand their frame of reference and what they are experiencing at this point in time.

A toxic culture can be one where people do not talk about their feelings. This is the case in engineering, a male-majority industry. We do not share what has been going on in our lives. We need to change that by challenging toxic masculinity and anchoring culture change efforts of DEI onto Health & Safety.

Because creating a psychologically safe culture where people can speak openly about what is going on in their lives is critical. If we can get this right, then this will help solve the high rates of suicidal ideation and self-harm within male-majority sectors and a new model of healthy masculinity will be shaped.

An Inclusive Operating System with Inclusive Interdependence© at the heart of it with SAFE Leaders© making the change.

Next Actions

This book is intended to lay the foundations of a working framework for creating psychological safety in the engineering industry, using the lessons from DEI and inclusive H&S to change the Operating System for greater cultural change. It also supports the ongoing ethical requirements and social responsibility of engineers, as outlined by the **Continuing Professional Development** (CPD)[56] and **Engineering Ethics Reference Group** (EERG),[57] which defines the following:

- **Respect for life, law, the environment, and public good**
  - Hold paramount the Health & Safety of others and draw attention to hazards
- **Leadership and communication**
  - Be aware of the issues that engineering and technology raise for society, and listen to the aspirations and concerns of others
  - Promote equality, diversity, and inclusion

I've collated what I've learned over my career in engineering and my experiences in trying to progress the conversation around DEI. Ideally, this book starts a dialogue and engages a community of professionals and practitioners who all want to work on redefining psychological safety and successful DEI practices.

---

[56] "Continuing Professional Development," Engineering Council, https://www.engc.org.uk/professional-development/continuing-professional-development-cpd/.

[57] "Statement of Ethical Principles," Engineering Ethics Reference Group, Engineering Council, 2017, https://www.engc.org.uk/standards-guidance/guidance/statement-of-ethical-principles/.

I'm hoping to engage in shared learning to evolve and merge my findings with other professionals interested in inclusive engineering – whether that's sociologists, behavioural scientists, psychologists, or any organisations interested in working on cross-sectional projects to leverage them for cultural change. If we all work together and embrace the intersectionality of thought, something greater can be achieved.

My vision for change comes down to embedding a mindset shift from the very beginning of an engineer's career. I want **students to use this book as a framework for their engineering design projects**, embracing the elements of DEI for a more inclusive future. I'd like lecturers and academics to make it a must-read alongside their standard curriculum.

I want organisations to understand the benefits to their businesses in terms of morale, productivity, and key performance indicators. And most of all, I want to **create parity between physical and mental health so we can change how the male majority views mental health**, themselves, and DEI in the workplace, which is key to saving lives.

> Create *parity* between physical and mental health so we can change how the male majority views mental health

When we engage the majority through helping them understand their own diversity story, we help everyone, inclusively. When we engage the majority using DEI and inclusive H&S to create psychological safety, *everyone* benefits and mental health across an entire organisation is improved.

Engineering has raised its game in promoting greater diversity in our profession. Even so, a lack of diversity remains in the engineering organisations taking charge. All too often, I see the same organisational logos and representatives appear at DEI events.

Of course, the efforts of these trailblazing organisations are to be applauded. Without them, we would not be moving forward at all. For example, many of our clients are doing a great job at supporting DEI both within their own organisations and through supply chains, and some also use it as a tool for public engagement. However, it is time for us to collectively move on from the early-adopters stage and reach a place where DEI adoption is a majority feature.

"DEI" is merely terminology. It is how we make sense of something that has always existed. It is intrinsic. We are simply putting words to nature's incidence, which we are increasingly exposed to through living in the age of globalisation. Sadly, we also live in a world where DEI is not a given. Some industries do better than others, but engineering and technology is not one of them.

The potential to shift gears and drive a new Operating System is a matter of perspective and psychological reasoning. Inclusion does not exist if an entire demographic is not included and represented. The importance of mental health does not count if the majority of those who die by suicide are not considered. And, however uncomfortable it may be to admit, DEI cannot thrive if the majority see no reason or benefit in implementing it. Opening these channels of communication invites experiential and empathetic learning to form a strategy that nurtures teams who care and look out for each other.

However, we cannot do this in a vacuum. We need thought leaders and fellow professionals to join us at EqualEngineers and create change across our entire industry. The more of us invested in updating an outdated Operating System towards Inclusive Interdependence, the brighter the future of engineering looks for *everyone,* and the more focussed we can be on solving the big global challenges we face that engineers play a critical role in addressing.

Dr. Mark McBride-Wright, MBE, CEng, MIChemE
Founder & CEO, EqualEngineers

EqualEngineers

Engineering inclusive cultures to attract, develop and retain talent

- ⊙ Mentoring Programmes
- ⊙ Training & Consultancy
- ⊙ Recruitment services
- ⊙ Awards & Events
- ⊙ And much more!

www.equalengineers.com

BIBLIOGRAPHY

Arata, Ray. *Showing Up: How Men Can Become Effective Allies in the Workplace.* New York: Diversion Books, 2022.

BCF Group. "History of Health & Safety." https://www.thebcfgroup.co.uk/health-and-safety-pages/history-health-safety-workplace.php.

Bonfield, Dawn. "Inclusive Engineering Framework." Towards Vision. https://www.inceng.org/inclusive-engineering-framework.html.

Brown, Jennifer. *How to Be an Inclusive Leader*, 2nd ed. San Francisco: Berrett-Koehler Publishers, 2022.

Business in the Community. "Mental Health at Work 2019: Time to Take Ownership." https://www.bitc.org.uk/report/mental-health-at-work-2019-time-to-take-ownership/.

Cambridge Online Dictionary. "Positive Action." https://dictionary.cambridge.org/us/dictionary/english/positive-action.

Cameron, Don. "History of Workplace Health and Safety." StaySafe. https://staysafeapp.com/blog/history-workplace-health-and-safety.

Cattermole, Jane. "Thames Water." MHFA England. https://mhfaengland.org/mhfa-centre/case-studies/thames-water/.

"Collective Intelligence: Number of Women in Group Linked to Effectiveness in Solving Difficult Problems." *Science Daily*. October 2, 2010. https://www.sciencedaily.com/releases/2010/09/100930143339.htm.

Creative Equity Toolkit. "Call Out and Call in Racism." https://creativeequitytoolkit.org/topic/anti-racism/call-out-call-in-racism.

Croner-i. "ConocoPhillips (UK) Ltd v Health and Safety Executive (2016) Court of Appeal 23 December." April 3, 2017. https://app.croneri.co.uk/law-and-guidance/case-reports/conocophillips-uk-ltd-v-health-and-safety-executive-2016-court-appeal.

Davidson Morris. "What Is Positive Discrimination?" June 25, 2021. https://www.davidsonmorris.com/positive-discrimination/.

Edmondson, Amy. "Psychological Safety and Learning Behavior in Work Teams." *Administrative Science Quarterly* 44, no. 2, (June 1999). https://doi.org/10.2307/2666999.

Edwards, David. and Mark McBride-Wright et al. "Inherent Safety: It's Common Sense, Now for Common Practice!", Hazards 25, Institution of Chemical Engineers, 2015, https://www.icheme.org/media/8500/xxv-paper-33.pdf

Ely, Robin J. and Debra E. Meyerson. "Unmasking Manly Men: The Organizational Reconstruction of Men's Identity." *Academy of Management*, November 30, 2017. https://doi.org/10.5465/ambpp.2006.27161322.

Engineering Council. "Continuing Professional Development." https://www.engc.org.uk/professional-development/continuing-professional-development-cpd/.

BIBLIOGRAPHY

Engineering Ethics Reference Group. "Statement of Ethical Principles." Engineering Council. 2017. https://www.engc.org.uk/standards-guidance/guidance/statement-of-ethical-principles/.

EngineeringUK. "Trends in the Engineering Workforce between 2010 and 2021." https://www.engineeringuk.com/media/318305/trends-in-the-engineering-workforce_engineeringuk_2022.pdf.

Government Equalities Office. "Equality Act 2010: A Quick Start Guide to Positive Action in Service Provision for Voluntary and Community Organisations." Equality and Diversity Forum. August 2010. https://assets.publishing.service.gov.uk/government/uploads/system/uploads/attachment_data/file/85026/vcs-positive-action.pdf.

Health & Safety Executive. "Health & Safety Statistics." https://www.hse.gov.uk/statistics/.

──────. "Lone Workers." https://www.hse.gov.uk/lone-working/worker/.

──────. "Reducing Error and Influencing Behaviour." https://www.hse.gov.uk/pubns/priced/hsg48.pdf.

Human Factors 101. "Getting Started." https://humanfactors101.com/getting-started/.

Lang, Nico. "Gen Z is the Queerest Generation According to New Survey." *Them*. February 24, 2021. https://www.them.us/story/gen-z-millennials-queerest-generation-gallup-poll.

Mackie, Stuart. "Record Fine for Alton Towers Health and Safety Failings." Thorntons Law. September 26, 2017. https://www.thorntons-law.co.uk/knowledge/record-fine-for-alton-towers-health-and-safety-failings.

Mayne, Mahalia. "Constant Stress and Zero Tolerance of Toxic Workplaces: What Gen Z and Millennials Really Think About Work." *People Management*. November 30, 2023. https://www.peoplemanagement.co.uk/article/1849539/constant-stress-zero-tolerance-toxic-workplaces-gen-z-millennials-really-think-work.

McBride-Wright, Mark. "Health & Safety: Diverse & Inclusive." *The Chemical Engineer Magazine*. July 20, 2017. https://www.thechemicalengineer.com/features/health-and-safety-diverse-and-inclusive/.

──────. "Masculinity in Engineering Research 2022." EqualEngineers. 2022. https://equalengineers.com/masculinity-in-engineering-report.

Mental Health First Aid. "About MHFA." https://www.mentalhealthfirstaid.org/about/.

──────. "ALGEE: How MHFA Helps You Respond in Crisis and Non-Crisis Situations." April 15, 2021. https://www.mentalhealthfirstaid.org/2021/04/algee-how-mhfa-helps-you-respond-in-crisis-and-non-crisis-situations/.

Mind. "What Is Self-Harm?" May, 2020, https://www.mind.org.uk/information-support/types-of-mental-health-problems/self-harm/about-self-harm/.

Mullany, Michael. "The Power of the Adoption Curve." LinkedIn post, April 18, 2018. https://www.linkedin.com/pulse/basics-adoption-curve-michael-mullany/.

Murugesu, Jason Arunn. "Men Predicted to Outnumber Women in Physics Until the Year 2158." *NewScientist*. January 11, 2023. https://www.newscientist.com/article/2354290-men-predicted-to-outnumber-women-in-physics-until-the-year-2158/.

———. "What Are Suicidal Feelings?" April, 2020. https://www.mind.org.uk/information-support/types-of-mental-health-problems/suicidal-feelings/about-suicidal-feelings/.

Occupational Safety and Health Administration. "Recording and Reporting of Occupational Injuries and Illnesses." https://www.osha.gov/laws-regs/regulations/standardnumber/1904/1904.7.

———. US Department of Labor. "State Plans." https://www.osha.gov/stateplans/.

Office for National Statistics. "Suicide by Occupation, England & Wales, 2011 to 2020 Registrations." https://www.ons.gov.uk/peoplepopulationandcommunity/birthsdeathsandmarriages/deaths/adhocs/13674suicidebyoccupationenglandandwales2011to2020registrations.

Peters, Steve. *The Chimp Paradox.* New York: TarcherPerigee, 2013. "Provost's Update: How Do We Manage Disagreement and Diverse Views in Our Community?" *UCL News*. March 22, 2023. https://www.ucl.ac.uk/news/2023/mar/provosts-update-how-do-we-manage-disagreement-and-diverse-views-our-community.

Sandroff, Ronni. "The History of Unions in the United States." Investopedia. September 1, 2022. https://www.investopedia.com/financial-edge/0113/the-history-of-unions-in-the-united-states.aspx.

Siddique, Haroon. "Male Construction Workers at Greatest Risk of Suicide, Study Finds." *The Guardian*. March 17, 2017. https://www.theguardian.com/society/2017/mar/17/male-construction-workers-greatest-risk-suicide-england-study-finds.

Talwar, Rohit. "STOP Cards Are Not Working! Why?" LinkedIn post, January 2021. https://www.linkedin.com/pulse/stop-cards-working-why-rohit-talwar.

UK Government. "Being Disability Confident." https://disabilityconfident.campaign.gov.uk/.

US Bureau of Labor Statistics. "7.8 Million Workers Had an Illness-Related Work Absence in January 2022." February 9, 2022. https://www.bls.gov/opub/ted/2022/7-8-million-workers-had-an-illness-related-work-absence-in-january-2022.htm.

Yoshino, Kenji. *Covering: The Hidden Assault on Our Civil Rights.* New York: Random House, 2007)

Zippia. "Engineer Demographics and Statistics in the US." https://www.zippia.com/engineer-jobs/demographics/.

Milton Keynes UK
Ingram Content Group UK Ltd.
UKHW022324280624
444841UK00006B/69